Governing Illinois

*Your connection
to state and local
government*

SECOND EDITION

Edited by
James M. Banovetz
Professor Emeritus of Political Science
Northern Illinois University

THE **INSTITUTE** FOR
PUBLIC AFFAIRS

University of Illinois at Springfield,
Springfield, Illinois

Library of Congress Cataloging-in-Publication Data

Governing Illinois : your connection to state and local government /
    edited by James M. Banovetz. -- 2nd ed.
        p.   cm.
    Includes index.
    ISBN 0-938943-16-2
    1. Illinois--Politics and government.   I. Banovetz, James M.
  JK5716.G68   1999
  320.4773--dc21

                                                                99-32266
                                                                    CIP

ISBN: 0-938943-16-2

This book is a revised edition of *Governing Illinois*, published in 1991 by *Illinois Issues*.

Developmental Editor: Rodd Whelpley
Cover and Text Designer: Diana L.C. Nelson
Photo Editor: Jill E. Barfield
Printer: United Graphics

Printed in the United States of America

10 9 8 7 6 5 4 3 2 1

The Institute for Public Affairs
P.O. Box 19234
University of Illinois at Springfield
Springfield, IL 62794-9243

Phone: 217-206-6502
Fax: 217-206-7257

e-mail: wojcicki@uis.edu

Web site: http://www.uius.edu/govern

On the Cover: Inside the Illinois State Capitol Dome, Springfield, Illinois.
Photographic art by Diana L.C. Nelson.

Contents

THIS SECOND EDITION

OF *GOVERNING ILLINOIS* IS DEDICATED TO

DARLENE EMMERT FISHER,

AN OUTSTANDING TEACHER

AND COLLEAGUE,

WHOSE PEDAGOGICAL INFLUENCE

HAS BEEN PRESERVED

AND EXPANDED

BY THE EXCELLENCE

OF HER CONTRIBUTIONS

TO THIS BOOK.

Foreword

Political philosophers writing about democracy agree that the maintenance of democracy requires an educated citizenry knowledgeable about government.

Past leaders of Illinois' governmental and educational systems have acknowledged the link between citizen education and successful democratic government. That link is the rationale for the state's long-established requirement that middle school and high school students demonstrate their knowledge of the Illinois Constitution and the state's system of government. It is also the rationale behind the development of this book about Illinois state and local government.

The first edition of *Governing Illinois*, published by *Illinois Issues* magazine in 1991, was designed and written for students in grades eight through twelve by some of Illinois' best teachers. Because it filled a critical educational need better than any other available materials, the first edition sold quickly. Some books were purchased by schools convinced that such a volume would enhance their social science/political science courses; others were bought by independent groups concerned with educating young citizens about Illinois state and local government. These organizations donated the books to local schools.

As Margaret Allan, Illinois Teacher of the Year, 1988-89, remarked about the book's first edition, "This book empowers students to become active participants in the political process. *Governing Illinois* is an exciting addition to the social studies classroom."

Laura Ryan and Ed Wojcicki have joined the same Illinois teachers who wrote the first edition, and together they have all done an even better job preparing this second edition. The contents of this book and its accompanying *Teacher's Guide* are as current and up-to-date as possible. But, in this information-rich era, we realize that words on a printed page can stay current for only so long. The principles of good government never go out of style. But politics is always on the move. To keep up with most current happenings in state and local government, the Institute for Public Affairs at the University of Illinois at Springfield, publishers of the second edition of *Governing Illinois*, have developed a web site to support the book. Check **www.uis.edu/govern** for chapter updates and links that expand the book far beyond the borders of these pages.

The publications staff at the Institute for Public Affairs at UIS join me in expressing our hope that this second edition will emulate its predecessor by bringing the story of Illinois state and local government to a growing number of students who will direct the future of our state in the 21st century.

James M. Banovetz, editor

Acknowledgments

The publications staff at the Institute for Public Affairs at the University of Illinois at Springfield has performed the Herculean task of moving this new edition through the publication process in time to be used in fall, 1999, school classes. Thanks go to: Institute Director **Nancy Ford** and the rest of the IPA Editorial Board; **Ed Wojcicki**, publisher; **Rodd Whelpley**, developmental editor; **Jill E. Barfield**, photo editor; and designer **Diana L.C. Nelson**. **Beverley Scobell** proofread early pages of the text. **Charlene Lambert** contributed her marketing expertise.

For their special assistance to the editor, thank you to **June Kubasiak**, office manager in the division of Public Administration at Northern Illinois University. Thanks also to **David Parish** for his insight early in the book's process and to **Randall Fritz**, whose quick, good work made the *Teacher's Guide* a valuable part of *Governing Illinois*.

Sara Stremsterfer, a teacher at Ursuline Academy at Springfield, gladly arranged a photo shoot, provided student models from her school, and encouraged student photographer **Vanessa VanHoudnos** to provide us photos in chapter 8. Thank you, too, **Dave Joens**, for taking original photos for chapter 9.

The Governing Illinois Second Edition Advisory Committee

Thanks go to the advisory committee for their guidance and encouragement in conceiving this edition of the text.

Margaret "Peggy" Allen
Illinois Teacher of the Year, 1988-89

Samuel K. Gove
Professor and director emeritus, Institute of Government and Public Affairs, University of Illinois at Urbana-Champaign

Joan W. Levy
Former president, Illinois Association of School Boards

Ann Pictor
Illinois State Board of Education

Jack Van Der Slik
Professor and director emeritus, Illinois Legislative Studies Center, Institute for Public Affairs, University of Illinois at Springfield

Illustration Credits

Our thanks to all those who contributed art and photography to this edition of *Governing Illinois*.

Chapter 1

The Illinois State Capitol

The Political Process: Parties, PACs, and Political Campaigns

by Patrick J. Burns

Frequently, news stories tell us that American students know little about their government. Such reports are usually accompanied by a listing of a few questions that students were unable to answer, such as: What great historic event occurred in the early 1860s? Who was the sixteenth president? In some cases Illinois students are asked to name their state legislators or to identify the subject matter of Article I of the Constitution of the State of Illinois. The implication of these reports is that all educated individuals should be able to answer these questions. Right now, you may be thinking, "I'll bet a lot of adults can't answer these questions either," or, "Who cares what happened in the 1860s or who the sixteenth president was?" It is impossible to remember all of the information contained in history books or government documents. If the students had been asked where answers to the questions could be found, the results of such surveys might have been different and perhaps more meaningful.

If the following headlines were in your local paper, would you be interested?

First offense brings loss of license for 90 days
House Passes Zero-Tolerance for Under-Age Drivers

School Board Votes No-Pass, No-Play, for Athletes

Two Year Limit on Welfare for Unwed Mothers under Consideration

Move in Legislature to Bar Teens From Riverboat Casinos

Other than the fact that all of these changes would affect students, what else do they have in common? All report actions taken by state or local governments.

Referring to the headlines, answer these questions:
- "What can I do if I disagree with school board policy?"
- "How can I have an impact on legislation that directly affects me?"

If you don't know the answer to these questions, you are not in position to stand up for your interests.

In a democracy such as ours, those who understand how the government works can make it work for them; those who do not understand how it works find that it often works against them. You have a choice of whether you are going to be one of the people who make things happen or one of those to whom things happen.

Power and Change

You may think that you have to be in a position of power before you can bring about changes. You may also feel that power is determined by money, skin color, or family background. While this view of power may have some truth, it is only partly true. If it were true today, Blacks could not attend schools with whites. They would sit in the back of the bus. They would not be served in "White" restaurants, and they would not hold political offices. All of these things were changed not by people in power, but by those who learned how to make government work for them. The people in power changed afterwards because of new civil rights laws and court decisions. Of course, in a democracy, change may take a long time and lots of coordinated effort.

Look at the students in your school. Are there girls wearing jeans? Do some boys have hair touching their collars? Are any of the boys wearing their shirt-tails outside their pants? Thirty years ago all of these were violations of the rules in most Illinois schools, and students who violated dress codes were subject to suspension. How many girls at your school participate in inter-scholastic athletics? There weren't many thirty years ago. Have any of you attended a rock concert? Rock concerts were banned in some cities thirty years ago. Student activists of the sixties worked hard to get those changes made. Find out what rights you

Lobbyists and members of the General Assembly meet at the brass rail along the Rotunda of the Capitol building in Springfield to count votes and discuss pending legislation.

already have as a student, because that is one of the first steps to understanding how government works. A good second step would be to make a list of changes you would like to see in your school and community.

Power and Politicians

Most of you are already aware of how state laws are written: Bills pass the legislature, are signed by the governor, and become law. Much more important to you, however, is understanding how to influence legislators and other government officials in order to pass or defeat bills.

To pressure legislators or other elected government officials, you first have to know what motivates them. Psychologists say that people want to be elected to a government office either because they enjoy feelings of power and prestige or because they enjoy helping others and wish to make the world a better place in which to live, or both.

Some of you may be thinking that an important reason was left out — money. While a desire for wealth may be a motivating factor for some people, money is not a factor for most. Today, most people who can get elected to office can easily earn more money in other occupations. Some people who seek public office have already established successful careers. Most elected offices are part-time, especially for a city or a county or other local governments. Some elective positions pay no salary at all. Members of your local school board are examples of people who, in many cases, receive no pay and usually serve from a sense of civic duty.

Politics is the art or science of influencing government; politics is also the art or science of winning election to a government office. Anyone holding an elected government position is also a politician. Some people enter politics and find that it is not at all what they expected. Perhaps they are uncomfortable using power, or they value their privacy more than the power and influence of the office. For whatever reason, these people do not continue in politics; however, for those who do enjoy politics and want to continue government service, their overriding goal becomes reelection. Special interest groups use politicians' desire for reelection as a means of trying to get them to do what they want them to do while in office.

A two-party system works best when there are overriding issues that separate the two parties. But when there are not, then candidates can break with the traditions of their party. In 1998, gubernatorial candidate George Ryan tried to reach beyond the regular Republican voting base by reaching out to more liberal groups such as gays and anti-gun activists. On the other hand, downstate Democratic candidate Glenn Poshard took conservative positions that seemed unusual to the more liberal Chicago Democrats.

Political Parties

To understand the workings of Illinois' political system, you must develop a knowledge of **partisan politics** in Illinois. Some say that the strong **two-party system** of Republicans vs. Democrats is our greatest political strength. It prevents the fragmentation of political power and the necessity of **coalitions** that occur in **multiple-party systems**. Others feel that it is our greatest weakness because many potential voters do not identify with either major party and become politically alienated.

A two-party system works best when there are overriding issues that separate the two parties. However, when there are many unrelated issues facing the voters, the voter may find that he or she agrees with one party on some issues and with the other party on other issues. This is particularly true in Illinois, where regional differences often separate the state on certain issues. For example, a downstate Republican and a downstate Democrat may find that they have more in common with each other than they do with their party counterparts in the suburbs or the inner city. Nevertheless, when the election is over, leaders of both parties are able to influence the votes of the elected representatives in the legislature.

U.S. census estimates from the late 1990s show that about 23 percent of Illinois' citizens and voters live in Chicago. Chicago votes Democratic, and the rest of Cook County, which has about 20 percent of Illinois' population, splits half and half between Democrats and Republicans. Thus, Cook County is dominated by Democrats. Another 21 percent of Illinoisans live in the affluent suburbs of the five "collar counties" around Cook — DuPage, Kane, Lake, McHenry, and Will — and vote mainly Republican. The remaining 36 percent live throughout the rest of the state in the other

Partisan politics The process whereby party leaders exert pressure on their party members in the General Assembly in order to get them to vote with the party on the legislation being considered.

Two-party system A political system made up of only two opposing parties. Other parties are either outlawed or strongly discouraged.

Coalition The temporary joining together of diverse groups to work together on a project, such as passing a piece of legislation.

Multi-party system A political system made up of several political parties. Usually, no single party will have a clear majority, so some of the parties must join together in a coalition to pass legislation.

96 counties. While Cook County has been a Democratic stronghold, the collar counties have been just as strongly Republican. In a statewide election, such as for governor or one of Illinois' U.S. senators, these two groups tend to neutralize each other, and the winner is determined by the rest of the state.

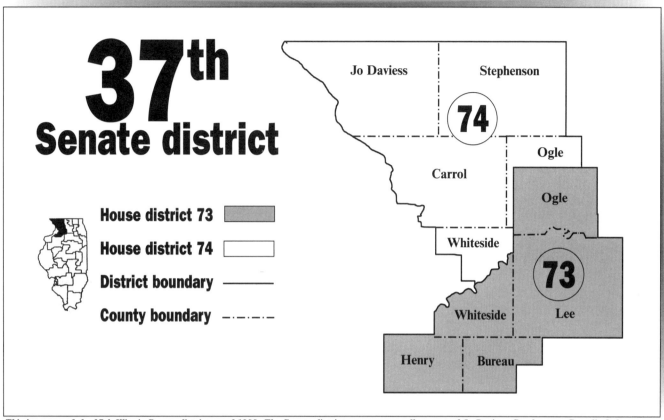

This is a map of the 37th Illinois Senate district as of 1999. The Senate district encompasses all or part of Jo Daviess, Stephenson, Carroll, Ogle, Whiteside, Lee, Henry, and Bureau counties. The map also shows how two House districts (the 73rd and 74th) are nested inside the Senate district. All people living in the area elect one state senator to represent them in the General Assembly. The people living in the 73rd House district (shaded on the map) elect one person to represent them in the Illinois House. The people living in the 74th House district elect another person to represent them in the Illinois House. After every national census (once every 10 years), the Senate and House district boundaries are redrawn so that each district contains about the same number of people.

Politics and Redistricting

Let's look at the rest of the state. First, remember that six counties around Chicago in northeastern Illinois have 64 percent of the state's people — and voters. The rest of the people in Illinois live in cities and towns and on farms spread from Rockford in the north to Cairo at the southern tip, from Quincy on the western border to Paris on the eastern border. Some areas are Democratic (like the Quad Cities and East St. Louis); others are Republican (like Peoria and Danville).

Now consider how members are elected to the Illinois **General Assembly**. The whole state is divided into fifty-nine **Senate districts**. The voters in each district elect a senator to the Illinois Senate. Each of the 59 districts is further divided in two, creating 118 **House districts**. Each of these elects one member to the Illinois House of Representatives. The boundaries for all these districts are redrawn every ten years after the U.S. census is taken, so each district is nearly equal in population. The creation of these districts is not a simple mathematical division of the population. It is done in the

General Assembly The legislature or law-making body of Illinois. It is made up of the House and the Senate.

Senate district One of 59 geographic divisions of the state from which a state senator is elected to the Senate chamber of the Illinois General Assembly.

House district One of 118 geographic divisions from which a state representative is elected to the House chamber of the Illinois General Assembly. Illinois House districts are nested so that two complete representative districts fall into the same geographic area as one of the state's Senate districts.

Special interest group A group of people sharing a common interest who organize in order to become involved in the political process.

Lobbyist Someone who tries to influence legislators to vote on issues the way a special interest group wants them to. Special interest groups can hire professional lobbyists, who, in Illinois, must register with the secretary of state.

PACs Political action committees (or PACs) are the campaign funding arms of special interest groups. They donate money to the campaign funds of candidates who vote for their interests or to the opponents of legislators who vote against their interests. Many donate heavily to legislative leaders, not individual candidates.

General Assembly by the Democrats and Republicans, who have all of the state population's voting records on computers. Democrats try to draw the boundaries to increase the likelihood of having more Democratic senators and representatives elected, so their party will control the state legislature. Of course, the Republicans try to do the same.

Special Interest Groups

The senators and representatives elected to the General Assembly have loyalties to their parties and are accountable to the people in their districts. In addition there are also the **special interest groups** that cut across the entire state — and nation.

Who are these special interest groups? They are made up of ordinary people sharing a common interest; they are usually headed by people who understand government and how the political system works and how to make it work for them. For example, your teacher is probably a member of a teachers' union: the Chicago Teachers Union or the Illinois Education Association/National Education Association (IEA/NEA) or the Illinois Federation of Teachers/American Federation of Teachers (IFT/AFT). These are special interest groups that work to influence politicians to support certain policies of interest to teachers, such as job security.

Many special interest groups operating in Illinois. Some are more influential than others. Among them are those representing manufacturers, insurance companies, retail merchants, farmers, highway contractors, the medical professions, liquor distributors, realtors, and organizations representing most professional and labor groups.

In addition, there are powerful interest groups that are built around a single issue or a combination of issues that have little or nothing to do with a business or occupation. Examples of these groups and their issues include:

- The National Rifle Association (NRA), which works for the right of citizens to have guns.
- The American Civil Liberties Union (ACLU), which works for the protection or expansion of personal freedoms.
- The American Association of Retired Persons (AARP), which works for economic benefits for retired workers.
- The Christian Coalition, which is involved with moral and religious issues.

Lobbyists and PACs

Many special interest groups recruit volunteer or hire professional **lobbyists**, and many form political action committees called **PACs**. In Illinois, all lobbyists and their organizations must register with the secretary of state. A lobbyist tries to influence legislators to vote on bills in a manner favorable to the organization he or she represents. Lobbyists provide a valuable service to legislators when they point out the advantages and disadvantages of various bills. They also help the legislator and other public officials by letting them know the desires of their constituents.

The PACs are the campaign funding arms of special interest groups. They use money and influence during election campaigns both to defeat candidates who vote against their interests and to help elect or reelect candidates who support their interests.

Many political scientists and political commentators are calling for laws that will prohibit or at least curtail the power of PACs. While PACs fit the concept of people working together to further their interests, unfortunately, many Americans have no PAC to represent their interests. These same Americans are often less politically active. As a result, their interests tend to be given less consideration.

Students in Illinois colleges have a lobby group in Springfield, but students in secondary and elementary schools do not. Without their own lobbyist or PAC, who then protects or expands rights for students in high schools, junior highs, and grade schools? Sometimes, some of the special interest groups and their PACs may indirectly support positions favorable to students. For example, the ACLU has argued in court to protect or expand student rights, and groups have argued for equitable school funding for all Illinois children. But often, no one lobbies specifically and solely on behalf of Illinois students.

Many of you may think getting a driver's license at age sixteen is the greatest event you can imagine. But at age eighteen you are granted a far greater power — the power to vote. Consider your future as a student in high school, college, or a business or trade school. Is there anything state government could do for you as a student? Public school students, represented by one giant organization, could become one of the state's largest special interest groups. Even if the students are not old enough to vote, with such a large number of students, modest dues would raise considerable money to hire a lobbyist and to fund a PAC. Such a lobby of even just Illinois eighth-grade students might be in a position to influence legislation such as financial aid, the minimum wage, and college entrance requirements.

Political Activity of Americans

Junior and senior high students are not the only group that has not formed a special interest group to protect or advance its interests. For example, unwed mothers have no organized special interest group. They and their children have been particularly vulnerable to the recent drive to cut welfare payments.

Why don't some groups participate? That's hard to answer, but demographic surveys show that voting and political activism increase with age, income, and education. The least politically active are likely to be young, poor, and dropouts. Some Americans never vote. They go through life without ever casting a ballot or even signing a petition or participating in a demonstration. Others vote regularly but take part in no other political activity such as contributing time or money to a candidate's campaign or to a political party or to a special interest group.

Constituents The people who an elected official represents.

Many Americans are not consistent in their political activity: They may vote in some elections but not in others; only occasionally may they be concerned or angry or upset enough to sign a petition, attend a board meeting, contact their legislator, participate in a rally, or contribute to a campaign or interest group. At the other end of the scale are political activists; they are deeply involved in political affairs on a regular basis. It should come as no surprise that legislation enacted into law today tends to favor the politically active and their interests because they have learned to make the system work for them.

Senator Dan Cronin of Elmhurst participates in debate before the vote is called on a 1998 bill before the Senate.

Leaders or Representatives

Lobbyists who represent interest groups with powerful PACs have access to politicians and will be able to influence their votes and other political actions. Even so, such lobbyists cannot be sure of getting what they want. Often the interests of one group clash with the interests of others. For example, an environmental interest group may want to ban throwaway bottles, but the bottling industry and retailers may oppose such a ban because it could cost them money. How does a legislator decide which way to vote when interest groups are opposed on an issue?

After listening to the various views concerning proposed legislation, individual legislators must make a choice. They consider the views of their party and the people in their district. What do the voters want? On some issues, the legislator may have very strong convictions. If the legislator feels very strongly, he or she will lead the fight for the bill even though it is unpopular with powerful special interests or the legislator's party leaders or even **constituents** in the district. In this instance, the legislator is functioning as a leader, rather than a representative. If legislators find themselves too often acting in opposition to positions taken by their party or interest groups that are powerful in their districts, they may find themselves in trouble during the next election.

Lobbyists know they will not win every legislator's vote; however, they cannot afford to lose too many votes or *they* may be out of a job. Lobbyists keep track of how legislators vote, and when reelection time comes, they have a list of "friends" and "enemies" ready for their PACs.

PACs and Campaigns

PACs flex their political muscle by giving campaign money to their legislator "friends." They recommend how their members should vote, and, in some cases, they encourage PAC members to perform campaign work for their political friends. Politicians who fail to support the position of the PAC will find that the campaign money and services will be withheld next time. Even worse, the money and services may be provided to their opponents.

It would be wrong to assume that PACs wait until the next election before they flex their political muscle. Just before important votes in the General

Assembly, the PACs representing special interest groups will have their members write letters and attend rallies in Springfield in favor of or opposed to legislation, depending on their position.

But any group, not just those with PACs, can write letters and rally.

Personal letters, faxes, phone calls, e-mails, and meetings have a major influence on politicians, whether they are state, local, or national. These methods added to rallies or demonstrations focus attention on an issue. Politicians in the General Assembly or on a city council, a county board, or a school board pay attention when citizens begin to show interest in an issue. An increase in political activity (letters, rallies, demonstrations) is a clue to the politician that continued and growing interest could mean citizens who did not vote in the last election will vote in the next. These additional voters could change the outcome of the next election.

Ticket-Splitting

From the time the state of Illinois adopted official ballots until 1997, voters could make one mark (or one punch) on a ballot and vote for all candidates of a political party. But a new law prohibited that method of straight-party voting. Voters still have the option of voting for every Democrat or every Republican on the ballot (or "ticket"), but they must punch each name individually. Today, however, a lot of people think of themselves as Independents. Many "split" their tickets by voting for some Democrats and some Republicans. Thus, party control of politics in Illinois is weaker than it has been in the past.

In the 1998 election of the legislators, Republicans retained control of the Illinois Senate, while the Democrats remained in control of the Illinois House. In statewide elections, Republicans captured four important state offices by electing the governor, lieutenant governor, attorney general, and treasurer. Democrats captured the offices of secretary of state and comptroller. Before the election, Republicans had held all of these offices.

Illinois has one Democratic U.S. senator, Dick Durbin, and one Republican senator, Peter Fitzgerald. In 1998, Fitzgerald defeated U.S. Senator Carol Moseley-Braun, the first Black woman elected to the U.S.

PACs — How Much and to Whom They Give

Traditionally, the top contributors to political campaigns in Illinois have been the political action committees of special interest groups. The table below shows that only two private corporations (the tobacco company Philip Morris and the phone company Ameritech) cracked the top 10 contributors list for 1995-1996, a time when restrictions on smoking and utility deregulation were hot issues.

Top 10 Contributors 1995-1996

To Republicans

1.	Illinois State Medical Society	$ 1,240,000
2.	Illinois Manufacturers' Association	$ 746,000
3.	Illinois Education Association	$ 584,000
4.	Illinois Hospital Association	$ 362,000
5.	Illinois Bankers Association	$ 307,000
6.	Illinois Realtors Association	$ 298,000
7.	Ameritech	$ 276,000
8.	Association of Beer Distributors	$ 273,000
9.	Philip Morris	$ 262,000
10.	Illinois Cable TV Association	$ 249,000

To Democrats

1.	Illinois Education Association	$ 682,000
2.	Illinois Trial Lawyers Association	$ 469,000
3.	Association of Federal, State, County & Municipal Employees	$ 286,000
4.	Illinois State Medical Society	$ 247,000
5.	Chicago Teachers Union	$ 226,000
6.	Illinois Federation of Teachers	$ 217,000
7.	Illinois Bankers Association	$ 200,000
8.	Association of Beer Distributors	$ 192,000
9.	Illinois Hospital Association	$ 187,000
10.	State AFL-CIO	$ 181,000

Source: The Sunshine Project, "Show Me the Money" brochure, 1998.

As you can see, some PACs and other organizations (the Illinois State Medical Society, the Illinois Education Association, and the Illinois Bankers Association, for example) give money to both Democrat and Republican candidates even though the philosophy of these interest groups may be more closely aligned to the philosophy of one or the other political party. Giving to candidates from both parties is a way for organizations to maintain ties to both parties, so that they end up backing whoever is in power. ■

Incumbent A person who already holds an elected office.

Senate. Her election back in 1992 was part of a trend to elect more women. In 1992, Moseley-Braun was supported not only by Blacks, but also by women's organizations in Illinois and around the nation. Her win was even more significant when you realize that, prior to defeating the Republican challenger, she unseated a veteran Democratic senator in the primary. This trend of women seeking high office seems to be holding. In 1996, Democrats nominated Comptroller Dawn Clark Netsch for governor and State Senator Penny Severns for lieutenant governor. But they were defeated by Governor Jim Edgar and Lieutenant Governor Bob Kustra.

In 1999, however, Corinne Wood, George Ryan's running mate, was sworn in as the state's first female lieutenant governor.

There are many men and women of all races who see no real difference between the two parties. The support for Ross Perot in the 1992 presidential election (and to a lesser extent in the 1996 presidential election) reflected this dissatisfaction with the two traditional parties. For a third party to compete, it must develop a strong grassroots organization and raise enough money to challenge. Many third parties simply can't do this for more than one or two elections.

In 1996 the General Assembly passed a law that prohibited "one-punch" voting. From 1818 up until 1997 voters could cast their vote for all of one party's candidates for office by punching one option on a ballot. Today, voters still have the option of voting for every Democrat or every Republican on the ballot (or "ticket"), but they must punch each name individually.

Campaigning for Reelection

Let's suppose a Democratic state senator with a strong pro-labor voting record is up for reelection in a district that could swing either Republican or Democrat. Both union- and business-oriented PACs will become involved in this race, as will the two political parties. This would be true even though **incumbents**, legislators who already hold office, are usually reelected. Incumbents have an edge because they are well known in their districts. In addition, incumbents are likely to receive money from the PACs that were reasonably satisfied with their voting records.

A challenger, on the other hand, must develop name recognition among the voters. At the same time, he or she must either convince some voters who voted for the incumbent in the last election to switch their votes or persuade enough people who usually don't vote to go vote. In this example, let's assume that Republicans and the business-oriented PACs will provide campaign money and services for the challenger. The first step in the challenger's campaign is to package and sell himself or herself to potential voters in much the same way products are advertised. Television and radio ads are key, since they can reach the most voters.

Frequently, a public relations firm will film the candidate and his or her family, trying to show that the candidate is interested in every voter in the district. If the district has a rural area, the candidate may be filmed wearing a seed company cap, leaning against some farm equipment, and talking to a group of farmers. If there are factories, the candidate may be filmed outside one wearing a jacket with a union logo. There can be other scenes: in front of an American flag, outside a church, on the street talking to members of the police force, or shooting baskets with a group of children. These scenes are put together, and a narrator's voice is recorded to add words to fit the idea of the pictures. The church and flag scenes reflect "good old-fashioned" morals and patriotism; the farm and factory scenes reflect understanding of the needs of farmers and workers; the scene with the policemen suggests a commitment to law enforcement and public safety; the basketball scene contains a reference to the American competitive spirit. It doesn't matter that the candidate attends church only once or twice a year, has no farm background, knows little about law enforcement, has never held a union card, or has no athletic ability. The incumbent, of course, will be doing the same things.

If you're thinking that this is dumb, that nobody would fall for this, remember commercials for products may seem dumb, too, but they generate sales. Just as a wise consumer will not be unduly influenced by advertising, you, as a wise voter, should not be unduly influenced by campaign commercials.

The Cost of Getting Elected

Running for the Illinois General Assembly is an expensive undertaking — and it's getting more expensive all the time. As you can see from the table below, very few candidates are able to finance an election with their own money. So, campaign contributors — individuals, corporations, and PACs — become very important to the candidates.

The Rising Cost of Running for the General Assembly

	Illinois House		Illinois Senate	
	1994	**1996**	**1994**	**1996**
Average spending by a candidate	$79,000	$99,000	$113,000	$146,000
Most spent by a candidate	$393,000	$485,000	$789,000	$758,000
Least spent by a winning candidate	$5,103	$109	$12,495	$8,271
Cost of the 10 most expensive races	$5.38million	$7.19million		
Cost of the 5 most expensive races			$3.16million	$5.29million

Source: The Sunshine Project, "Show Me the Money" brochure, 1998.

Selling their own candidate is often not enough. PACs and parties may also attack the opponent through negative campaigning. They will investigate the senator and his or her family for any evidence of wrongdoing. They will look at the candidate's voting record for inconsistencies and for votes on issues that could draw another special interest PAC into campaigning against the senator. If found, the information is turned over to friendly reporters. For example, a vote for handgun registration could bring in the National Rifle Association. One relatively new technique is to find a particularly unfavorable photo of the incumbent and use it in contrast to the best possible photo or film clip of the challenger.

Everything described so far is legal and acceptable campaign practice, but some campaign managers resort to what are called "dirty tricks." If they find no evidence of wrongdoing, they manufacture some against the opponent. Campaign workers spread these derogatory rumors or charges about the opponent by word of mouth, claiming they come from an unnamed but very knowledgeable source.

Campaign Issues

You will note that so far nothing has been said about the issues of labor and management in this imaginary campaign. Political campaigns do not often deal with in-depth discussions of the issues. The price of ads in the media makes it quite expensive for a candidate to cover any topic in detail.

SUM IT UP

There are many players in the political process in Illinois. They are

- political parties,
- party leaders,
- special interest groups,
- PACs,
- elected representatives, and
- voters.

You, as a citizen, are now, or soon will be, able to participate in the process at one level or another. While some of you may eventually seek elective office and a leadership position, others may choose to work behind the scenes. Some of you may prefer to work with a special interest group rather than getting involved with a particular political party. Now is the time to become involved, and the best place to start is at the local level. Look around you. Are there things you would like so see changed? If so, get involved! Get your friends involved! You must understand that you will not win every time. You will not always be able to bring about those changes that you desire; however, in the process of becoming involved in the political process you will learn how the system works and find out how you can make it work for you. ■

To find out more...
start with the *Governing Illinois* web site at **www.uis.edu/govern**

News reports in the media may be very brief and served up in small doses called sound bites. Candidates also tend to make the same speeches, tailoring them for different audiences but providing only sound bites to report in newspapers or on the radio or television. So the process of mass communication doesn't lend itself to full coverage of the issues.

Also, voters like to hear that problems can be solved without sacrifice on their part, and campaigners tell voters what they like to hear. After the election, when problems remain or sacrifices are demanded, voters lose trust in campaign promises. During past elections, voters were told that more prisons and tougher sentencing would put a stop to crime. The new prisons are full; new jobs were created in construction and criminal justice; business firms profited from contracts. Crime rates are down. But it has not completely gone away.

In the past, voters were told that the state lottery would provide plenty of funding for schools. But schools remained underfunded. Then, special interest groups advocated gambling casinos as the new answer to funding education and other local projects. But schools remained underfunded. In 1994, one candidate for governor, Democrat Dawn Clark Netsch, took the unusual position of calling for a tax increase to fund public schools. Conventional wisdom says asking for a tax increase is a "kiss of death" to a politician. She surprised political experts by winning the Democratic primary; however, in the general election she lost to incumbent Governor Jim Edgar by one of the largest margins ever. Ironically, in Edgar's second term, he came out in favor of a school funding plan that was remarkably similar to the one Netsch campaigned on in 1994. ■

Chapter 2

Illinois students celebrate Statehood Day with a visit to the Old State Capitol in Springfield.

The Powers and Duties of Government: How People Fit In

by Eleanor Meyer

Take a look at the headlines in your daily paper. You may be surprised to discover how much of the news has to do with something that was done by the government. It might be something that was done by the government in your community — your local government. Or, it could be news of a decision that was made by the General Assembly in

Federal government The central government in a system in which state governments recognize the authority of a higher government. In the case of the United States, the federal government is the president, the Congress and the Supreme Court and agencies of those bodies.

Democracy A government by the people that is exercised directly by the people (where all vote on every issue) or through elected representatives (where the people elect someone to vote for them in a governing body, such as the Illinois General Assembly).

Springfield—your state government. Much of the news deals with issues that are the business of the national or **federal government.** These decisions are made in Washington, D.C. All Americans are subject to the rules established by these three levels of government, and all the governments are subject to the citizens who vote. This book focuses chiefly on your state government and the many ways in which it affects your life.

Maybe you're thinking, "I don't read newspapers for news. I only read the sports section and the comics." Or you might be saying to yourself, "Who cares about the government? It's boring." Yet the government has influence in almost every aspect of your life. It is through the media—newspapers, television, radio, magazines, and the Internet — that citizens can be informed about government activities.

If the government could control the media, we would only see and hear about the things the government wanted us to know. Freedom of the press, therefore, is one of our most cherished rights. Thomas Jefferson felt so strongly about freedom of the press that he said, "Were it left to me to decide whether we should have a government without newspapers, or newspapers without government, I should not hesitate a moment to prefer the latter."

This book was written with the hope that you will develop new attitudes about government. It is important for

To some, the government may seem as remote and impersonal as the Illinois State Capitol Building. If you have some of those ideas about your government, you need to get a clearer picture of what government is all about.

you to realize that government affects your life every day in every way. Once you understand the importance of government, you will see why **democracy** is only truly successful when all of its citizens are aware of the important part they must play in making that government work. If this book is truly successful, you will want to become involved and participate in the democratic process right away rather than at some vague time in the future.

Illinois State Government

The state government of Illinois. What do those words mean to you? Is the state government something that you know is real, but seems far away? Is it a vague idea in your mind about a group of people who meet in Springfield and make decisions about things that you don't think you understand? Perhaps you think of government as a place — a place where laws are made and taxes are collected and spent. Or do you think of state government as "those politicians" in Springfield who haggle and argue a lot and who don't seem to get anything done until the last few days of their spring session that ends in May or sometimes stretches into June?

If you have some of those ideas about your government, it means that you need to get a clearer picture of what government is all about. You need a way to make it seem less complicated. So let's begin with why we need government in the first place.

Why Do We Need Government?

Stop for a moment and think about what your classroom would be like if there were no rules about your attendance, your promptness, your participation, your conduct, or your supplies. What if there were no regulations to control the length of the class, the course requirements, the number of students in the room, or the professional training of your teacher? Pretty soon a state of chaos would erupt, right? If you belong to a ball team or a club at school, rules govern your participation. Common sense tells us that without rules time is wasted, work is not done, goals are not attained, and confusion reigns.

Running the state is somewhat similar to running the classroom or the school. In a way, you and your classmates are a microcosm of the state. A microcosm is a little world that is typical of a larger world. The students in your class are a mixture of people of different sizes, shapes, and backgrounds. They have different cultural heritages and beliefs and different desires and attitudes. The same is true of the rest of the people in Illinois, and there are over twelve million of them. Just as your school would be a mess if there were no rules and regulations to guide people, the state would be very disordered without some plan for managing it.

That is what state government does. It provides a plan and a set of rules for everyone who lives in Illinois. Someone needs to set standards, for example, for such things as water treatment (to be sure that we have clean water to drink), sewage disposal (to be sure our sewage does not make people sick), and education (to see that education is available to every person of school age). It simply makes sense for the state government, which acts on behalf of all the people, to do these jobs. The state also establishes criminal codes as a means of regulating individual behavior.

The government, in turn, must also operate under a set of rules to make sure it does what the people want. Maybe the Constitution of the State of Illinois will seem less complicated to you if you think of it as the set of rules under which the government operates. That Constitution was writ-

The government sets the standards for things such as water treatment, sewage disposal, and education. Here, Illinois Environmental Protection Agency field inspectors are assessing a wastewater treatment facility.

Delegate A person authorized to represent another person or group of people.

Executive branch One of three branches of Illinois state government. This branch is charged with carrying out the laws enacted by the legislative branch.

Legislative branch One of three branches of Illinois state government. This branch is charged with creating state laws.

Judicial branch One of three branches of Illinois state government. This branch is charged with interpreting and enforcing the state's laws and rules.

District A geographic division from which representatives are elected. For Illinois state government, there are 59 Senate districts and 118 House districts.

Deficit A monetary shortfall caused by spending more money than is currently being received.

Lobbyist Someone who tries to influence legislators to vote on issues the way a special interest group wants them to. Special interest groups can hire professional lobbyists, who, in Illinois, must register with the secretary of state.

ten by people elected as **delegates** from across the state, and the Illinois Constitution was ratified or approved by its citizens in a statewide election.

How Are Decisions Made?

The rules in the Illinois Constitution provide us with guidelines for running our representative government in Illinois. There are powers and duties assigned to the **executive**, **legislative**, and **judicial** branches, just as there are in the U.S. Constitution for the federal government. The voters in your **district** elect a representative and a senator to go to Springfield to work for your interests, just as they elect someone to go to Washington, D.C., to work for the interests of Illinois in the U.S. Congress.

But don't forget, when the Illinois General Assembly makes decisions, it makes them for all the people in all the districts, and the state representatives and state senators often have tough choices to make. Maybe your student council has been in a similar situation. They had successful fundraisers, and then they had to decide how to use the money. Some members may have wanted to buy computer equipment, others may have wanted lab equipment, and perhaps some thought they deserved to spend some of the money on themselves. Any representative group will spend time debating, arguing, soul searching, and finally, compromising, before the final vote is taken.

Think how much more complicated a state legislator's job must be, especially in a state as diverse as Illinois. Illinois is both agricultural and industrial; it is urban and rural; it is cosmopolitan and provincial. It has great wealth as well as areas of great poverty. Each district in the state has special needs for which it wants state help. Your home district might need money for new roads while another might want a prison built so that new jobs will be created. Some areas of the state desperately need more money to keep their schools going. The list of demands is long. Yet the state cannot spend money it does not have.

What if everyone in your family had the same birthday? What would be the chance of your getting the presents you wanted? In a way, that's the way people are about their government. They expect the government to give them what they want, and they expect their representatives to find a way to get it, even though the people who live in other districts are also pressuring their representatives to bring home the goods for them.

When the Illinois General Assembly makes decisions, it makes them for all the people in all the districts, and the state representatives and state senators often have tough choices to make. Here, Senator Walter Dudycz of Chicago discusses pending legislation with lobbyists.

Deciding Where the Money Goes

There's more to it. In addition to trying to meet the needs of all regions of the state, the General Assembly must make its decisions with a budget in mind. There is just so much money to spend but many, many ways to spend it. You've seen those pie graphs that show how much money is available and where it goes.

You might appreciate how tough it is to decide how to allocate all that money if you would use your imagination and turn that budget into a pizza. Put yourself in the impossible situation of having to feed twenty-five people with a pizza that is large enough for just twelve servings. How do you decide who gets a slice? Do you give the most to those who are pushiest? Do you deny it to those who got there late? Do you cut it up in very small pieces so that everyone gets some but no one really satisfies his or her appetite?

The demands on the state budget are many. It may help to think of the state budget as a 12-serving pizza that must somehow feed 25 people. Making decisions on how to divide it is difficult work.

The state budget is like that pizza. Just as there is only so much pizza to be divided, there is only so much money to be divided by the government. While the national government has often operated with a **deficit**, that is, it spends more money than it takes in during a year, the state and local governments cannot do that. Article VIII of the Illinois Constitution requires that state government's spending plan for one year cannot exceed state government's estimate of the money it will get in that year. Citizens must realize that the state government cannot solve all problems by spending more money—it can only spend the money it receives in a year, mainly from taxes paid by citizens. If government spends more, it must tax more, and raising taxes is something that politicians usually don't want to do.

Determining how to divide the money in the state budget is something like the problems with the pizza. There is just so much money to spend. There are hundreds of ways to divide it. There are **lobbyists** who try to persuade legislators to spend it for their special interest group. Those groups might include farmers, lawyers, doctors, insurance companies, health agencies, welfare recipients, teachers.

There are 118 representatives and 59 senators who are responsible for making the budget decisions. They should keep in mind what the Preamble to the Illinois Constitution says about providing "for the health, safety and welfare of the people" and about eliminating "poverty and inequality" and about assuring "legal, social, and economic justice." If you were a legislator, how would you decide to vote if you had to choose between providing aid to the ever growing numbers of elderly citizens who need long-term health care and the growing demand for government-funded day care for children of working mothers? Which group would support you in the next election because of the way you voted?

Government of the People, by the People, and for the People

Do you still think government is boring? Are you at least beginning to see that it is not some vague "thing"; it is people, and they are very real and very active. Every **bill** that is passed into law by the General Assembly and signed by the governor begins with the words, "Be it enacted by the people of Illinois, represented in the General Assembly:" This reminds us that the legislature is doing its business with the consent of the governed, that is, the citizens of Illinois. It reminds us, as Abraham Lincoln did over 100 years ago in his Gettysburg Address, that this truly is a government "of the people, by the people, and for the people." Those words are meaningless if the people — you — do not think it is important to understand how the system works.

Government Enters Your Life

Let's look at some of the ways in which government directly affects your life. You started school at the age that is set by the state. If you attended preschool or nursery school, the state had rules about how that school was run. People who run such schools have to be licensed by the state. To attend school, you had to be inoculated against certain contagious diseases. This protects not only you; it protects the rest of society as well because you will not be a carrier of those diseases. If you participate in any school athletic programs, you know that you had to have a physical exam before you could play. It's the law.

You may question the state's right to interfere in your personal life, but remember, the Preamble to the Illinois Constitution says that we are committed to "provide for the health, safety and welfare of the people." Since the law requires you to attend school, the school is an ideal place in which to reach all of the children and to take steps to protect their health.

The government also has some control over what you should be taught in school. Just as this class is designed to educate you to understand and appreciate your system of government, the school must offer health classes that point out the risks involved in experimenting with drugs and using tobacco and alcoholic beverages. Addiction to drugs not only affects health; it also leads to crime and the breakdown of family. All of society suffers when its families, and especially its children, are in trouble. Many teenagers, as you know, are becoming parents too soon. By providing information to students at an early age, the state hopes to help young people to make wise choices even though they live in a world in which drinking, smoking, taking drugs, and engaging in sex are sometimes made pretty appealing on TV and in movies and magazines. But the information that young people pick up in these state-mandated health classes may indeed be having a positive social affect. A report by the Annie E. Casey Foundation was released in 1998. It revealed that the rate of births to teenage mothers in Illinois decreased by 12 percent between 1991 and 1996. The report showed that the percentage of teenagers in the U.S. who have had sex dropped from 54 percent in 1990 to 48 percent in 1997.

So, while each individual has wide freedom to choose the lifestyle he or she wants, society can provide the means for helping people make an educated choice. In a democratic society, where the powers of its government are derived from its citizens, it is important for the citizens to be literate and able to support themselves.

Government and Your Health

The government plays a much bigger role in health care than most teenagers may realize. There is much talk of health care reform, and there is a real need for this reform as legislators look to the future. Why? There is a very large generation of Americans known as **baby boomers**. When they retire in the next ten years or so, there will be fewer Americans working, and that means there will be fewer paycheck deductions to help finance **Medicare**. The program could go broke. One step towards solving

A home health care nurse checks up on an elderly patient. Programs like Medicare that help provide health insurance for people 65 and older are financed by the government through taxes on income.

the problem was taken through the 1997 Balanced Budget Act. The U.S. Congress responded to cries for a balanced budget and for Medicare reform by reducing the amount of funding for Medicare. It sounds like the right thing to do, doesn't it? Unfortunately, solutions often lead to new problems.

The reduced Medicare payments led to some alarming news items. On December 26, 1998, Associated Press reporter Ann Love filed a report that said: "Inadequate Medicare payments are the reason health plans will drop more than 400,000 elderly and disabled patients next year." Drop them. Are you shocked? Read on. In December 1997, the *Chicago Tribune* reported: "In the last 15 months, between 850 and 1,200 Medicare-certified home health agencies — or nearly 1 out of every 10 agencies in the nation — have closed, citing stingy government payments." It's a tough problem. You see, demand for home care services has increased greatly, partly because medical technology has made it possible for more people to be cared for at home rather than in more expensive long-term care nursing homes. Now that there are tighter controls for the amount that Medicare will pay for these services, there is a public outcry for stopping this reform. Does it seem contradictory that people want reform, but they don't want it to affect them? If you were a legislator, how would you reform Medicare? How would you respond to lobbyists who are trying to protect the health needs of the elderly and the disabled? What plans would you suggest for preventing a total collapse of Medicare in the next 10 years when 76 million baby boomers begin to retire? It's quite a dilemma, and it is an issue that will be in the news for some time.

Don't Take My Driver's License!

If you still cannot see that government influences your life every day, it might help to think about one of your cherished possessions — your driver's license. Even if you are not yet old enough to drive, you probably have day-dreamed about getting behind the wheel and taking off — legally. Since driving is a serious responsibility, the government has determined that you must be 16 years of age before you take the tests that allow you the privilege of owning a driver's license. Of course, there are rules to be followed so that the roads and highways are safe for all citizens. There are state, county, and local police to enforce these rules. All of this comes under the responsibility of government.

When some of these rules are violated too often, the state government, which issues driver's licenses, has the authority to tighten up the regulations. For instance, in Illinois the legal drinking age for beer and wine used to be 19. When statistics showed that an overwhelming number of auto accidents were the result of teenage drinking and driving, the state, acting in the interest of the safety of all its citizens, changed the drinking age to 21 in 1980. In 1994, the General Assembly passed a bill that approved an immediate three-month license suspension for anyone under age 21 who is caught driving with alcohol in his or her blood. A second offense would mean a one-year suspension of the driver's license. Also, the state introduced graduated licensing in 1998. Under this law, persons under 18 must spend 25 hours of behind-the-wheel driving practice with an adult in the car before becoming eligible for a driver's license. This is in addition to the six hours of training provided in driver education class. There are other regulations with regard to your learner's permit, the number of passengers that can travel with you, the use of seat belts, and penalties for moving violations in a two-year period. These are clear examples of state government making provisions for the safety and welfare of the people.

Finally, your license is not handed to you just because you passed driver's training. You must pay a fee for it, just as you had to pay for the permit that allowed you to take the instructions. The money that you pay when you get a license is one of the legitimate ways in which the government is able to raise money to do some of the things that it is expected to do.

The money from these fees is spent in many ways: It helps pay for the cost of testing applicants for driver's licenses, but some of the money is also used to help pay for such government services as the construction and repair of roads, driver education programs, and bicycle safety training programs. None of the money goes directly to the persons who conduct the driver's license tests or who issue your license to you. The money goes to the state treasury, and the salaries of these state workers, like all state employ-

If you still cannot see that government influences your life every day, it might help to think about one of your cherished possessions — your driver's license.

ees, are set by laws and rules.

The state Constitution gives the Illinois General Assembly the power to raise money in various ways. Licensing fees, fines, user fees, and proceeds from the sale of state resources are all sources of funds, but taxes on what you buy (sales taxes) and on what you earn on a job (income taxes) are the major sources of money for state government. Local governments have the power to tax property. You will learn more about taxes in chapter 8. There is an old saying that we can be certain of only two things in life — death and taxes. Nobody likes to pay taxes, but most citizens realize that we have to pay for all the services that we expect from our governments. Remember that pizza?

Medicaid A joint federal, state, and municipal program that provides medical assistance for persons with low incomes and limited assets.

How Tax Dollars Reach Your Community

What are some of these services that people want and how do they reach from Springfield to your hometown? Before we answer that, it might help to think about the many categories of people in any community. There are children and adults. There are students, workers, and retired people (who may also be students). There are business people, farmers, veterans, **Medicaid** recipients, alcoholics, drug abusers, child abusers, other lawbreakers, and on and on. While every community may have its schools, restaurants, nursing homes, and stores, it may also have specialized services. Some have big shopping centers; others have large industries; some are farming communities, while others are centers for banking and professional services; still others have universities, hospitals, tourist attractions, or prisons. You get the idea—there is a great deal of variety and activity in every corner of Illinois.

What you may not realize, though, is that for all of those groups we just listed, some government agency or department is responsible for regulating, counseling, inspecting, or providing some type of service. Each of these agencies has offices and staffs. They print brochures and other materials to let the public know what is available through their offices. They might sound familiar when we tell you that these departments have names like Department of Agriculture, Department on Aging, Department of Children and Family Services, Department of Corrections. These are just a sample. Your teacher probably has a copy of the *Handbook of Illinois Government*, which tells more about them. (It is published by the Illinois secretary of state.) You can also read more about them in chapter 5 on the executive branch.

The point is, these departments may have offshoots in your town or city, but you may not recognize them as part of the government. If your community offers programs on alcohol and drug abuse, if it provides homes for foster children, or if it gives assistance in the form of nursing care and meals for the elderly, then it is making use of state funds to provide for the "health, safety and welfare of the people."

Sometimes the state provides these services directly. For example, the state has hospitals that care for the mentally ill. Other times the state provides these services through a local government. Your county, for example, has a department of public aid to help the poor, and it is likely that a not-for-profit agency, such as a senior citizens center, provides programs to help elderly citizens. The idea is to make government services more readily available across the state.

The Three Main Levels of Government

There are many governments and government offices in Illinois, but they all fall into the three main levels — federal, state, and local. It might help you to think about them as if they were the floors of a three-story building. The ground floor represents your local government. In a **municipality**, this might be a mayor and a city council or a village board of trustees. For your county it will be a county board that meets in the county seat. There are lots of other local governments on that ground floor in Illinois: townships, school districts, library districts, and airport authorities, for example. All are governments located in the community and run by local citizens. You'll learn more about local governments in chapter 7.

The second floor of the building represents the state government. The state government offers some services directly. For example, it builds state highways and operates the prison system. State government also coordinates the efforts of local governments to be sure that other services such as public education are made available to every person in the state. The state government is the link between the bottom floor and the third, or top floor, which is the national, or federal, government.

The federal government on the top floor also has certain powers and responsibilities. For example, it provides military protection, maintains our relationships with other nations, and helps state and local governments provide financing for housing, health, welfare, education, and many other programs for people.

The three floors of government are connected by stairs or elevators just as the three levels of government are linked through many of the agencies and departments that we have been talking about. Each floor supports the other, and the top floor would collapse without the support of the other two floors: The federal system would collapse without the support and participation of the people throughout the nation.

While it would still be possible for a single national government to run this country, it would be far less desirable than our federal system that leaves certain matters in the hands of citizens in the states and communities. If

If your community provides homes for foster children, then it is making use of state funds to provide for the "health, safety and welfare of the people."

only a centralized national government existed, you would have to picture a huge building with no floors between the roof and the ground floor. There would be a vast space between bottom and top, just as there would be a great distance between local communities and their national government. Other nations don't have state governments. All powers reside in the central, national government, as in England.

These three levels of government sometimes affect your life in unlikely ways, and we are trying to convince you that you should care about that.

Government Regulations and Politics Are Everywhere

Government sets standards for water treatment plants, sanitary districts, pesticide use, utility rates, building and highway construction, to name a few. Even cemeteries are governed by certain burial procedures! Actually, about 75 percent of the activities of your local government must comply with state and federal regulations.

The case study on pages 26-32 illustrates how one area of the state is working through many government agencies at the local, state, and federal levels in order to comply with the regulations associated with the seemingly simple task of getting rid of garbage. In addition to the legal factors involved with a problem such as this, there are also political considerations: First, who wants to live near a landfill? Second, who is going to vote for an official who brings a landfill to his or her community? The problem of garbage — like so many other problems — is more complicated than it first appears.

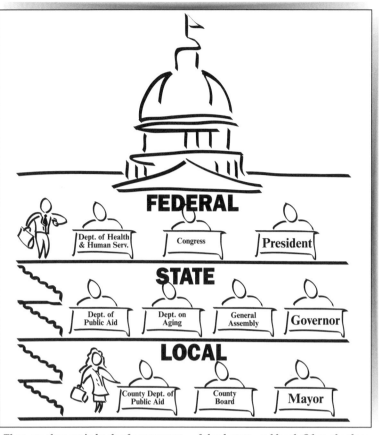

There are three main levels of government — federal, state, and local. Often, the three levels must coordinate efforts to give people the services they want. For example, the federal Department of Health and Human Services might provide funding for a health program. The state Department of Public Aid might then coordinate the efforts of the county departments of public aid that would make sure that the health services reached the people of each Illinois county participating in the federal program.

Problems Lead to Solutions

The case study at the end of this chapter is just one example of how the three levels of government affect all of us, every day, in a very basic way. We use the example of trash disposal to illustrate the three levels of government because it is a problem that will still be around when you are old enough to vote. It is a national problem.

People are working on solutions to the problem, though, and government can help by providing money for research. Recycling centers are part of the solution. In Illinois, corn-based degradable plastic bags for solid waste disposal are being used in some cities. This solution has the added benefit of providing a new market for Illinois farmers.

But, sometimes we discover that the solution to one problem leads to the creation of another. Here is an example of such a situation. In response to

NIMBY An abbreviated term that stands for "not in my back yard." NIMBY describes the attitude that some citizens take when they oppose an idea not necessarily because it is bad but because it will affect the value of their property.

the shortage of landfill space, some people have proposed the building of waste-to-energy incinerators. These are plants that burn large quantities of waste materials and generate electrical energy in the process. At first glance, these plants solve several problems.

First, they provide an economic boost to struggling communities by generating construction jobs, permanent jobs, fees for accepting the waste of other communities, and an increase in tax dollars. So far, so good. In addition, these plants would generate power, which would be sold to local power companies, thereby reducing the amount of coal that is burned to meet the demand for electricity.

Recycling centers have become part of the solution to the state's waste disposal problems.

The amount of garbage needed to be burned to consistently generate electric power — perhaps as much as 1,800 tons per day — is easily obtained from municipal areas such as Chicago. The city has no more space for landfills. So, companies in smaller cities could take Chicago's garbage and generate income from it by converting the waste to energy. These cities would generate income by taxing the profits these companies would earn.

NIMBY as a Roadblock to Change

But let's say a waste-to-energy incinerator is proposed in the Chicago suburbs. There would almost certainly be opposition from concerned citizens. How could anyone disagree with plans that seem to provide a perfect solution to a major problem?

First of all, opponents would see no reason to take care of Chicago's garbage. They are part of the NIMBY problem. **NIMBY** stands for "not in my back yard." NIMBY describes the position that some property owners — and even entire communities — may take when they hear that the government wants to allow something they don't like — such as a waste disposal facility or a mega-hog farm — to operate in their area.

In this case, waste facility critics may also reject the plan because the success of these plants depends on huge amounts of garbage being burned on a daily basis. Thus, it encourages the accumulation of waste at a time when people are being encouraged to reduce waste.

Second, concerned citizens do not want to take the risk of having even small amounts of hazardous emissions accumulating in the soil, air, and water of their community. They argue that no one can predict what the long-term effects might be.

Finally, there is the problem of what will be done with the fly ash that remains after incineration. Is it safe? In 1994, the Supreme Court ruled that waste-to-energy plants must treat the ash they produce as hazardous waste if it contains any dangerous materials. Opponents want to know how plant developers plan to dispose of this new form of waste.

So, you see, problem solving is not always an easy task. And this particular issue, by the way, involves all three levels of government. Usually, it is the local government, such as the city council, that approves a plan to build an incinerator in a community. This approval comes after a presentation by the developer, the local economic development committee, and public hearings. The builder must meet both state and federal regulations for protecting the environment. Then, the Supreme Court—the highest authority in the country—made the ruling on hazardous waste that further affects the disposal process.

In most cases, opposition to these incinerators has come from those citizens who insist on exercising their right to raise questions and express disapproval of such plants. If such people did not address the issue, developers and business interests would proceed with their plans and might even be less concerned with safety issues.

Do You Want Progress or Not?

Just as it is easy to take our garbage collection for granted, it is easy to expect our roads and highways to be built and maintained for our convenience. Our nation is automobile dependent. Look at the state highway map and see the countless number of roads that crisscross Illinois. Billions of dollars are spent to build and maintain this system. All of the funding comes from government — local, state, and federal.

Although the Tenth Amendment to the U.S. Constitution clearly gives states the right to make laws affecting their people, there are times when the federal government can use its muscle to influence state legislation. For example, if state laws do not comply with the federal government's laws on maximum speed limits or minimum drinking ages, the federal government can withhold funds for highway construction. The state could set a higher speed limit or lower its drinking age, but it would then have to build all of its roads with its own money. No state can afford to lose this help. This is another example of state and federal powers.

The need for more highways creates some problems that are similar to the problems that accompany the need for more landfill sites. Many areas of this country are developing rapidly, and state and county officials try to ease the increasing traffic volume by working to enlarge two-lane roads to four-lane roads. That sounds reasonable enough, right? Yet the NIMBY attitude pops up again because there are many citizens who don't want the increased growth in their communities and neighborhoods.

There is continuing conflict between those who see growth and development as a positive force called progress and those who don't want growth and development because of problems they may cause. The debate may focus on new construction and jobs versus loss of open space and increased traffic congestion. Many people do not want to live on a four-lane road and will fight any attempt to make their street wider. Are you beginning to understand how difficult it can be for legislators to make decisions that satisfy people and at the same time protect the rights and meet the needs of people? We're back to dividing up that pizza again. ■

SUM IT UP

By now, you should have a clearer idea of the ways in which government influences your life — every day. We live under a system of government that operates on three levels — local, state, and federal. These governing bodies must work within a budget, and they make decisions that touch upon many aspects of our lives — decisions about our schools, health care, licensing, and even trash disposal. At times, the programs that the government establishes run into problems. Public outcry often forces legislators to find solutions to these problems. However, solutions often create new problems, like the ones you read about with regard to landfills and Medicare reform.

The chapters that follow will help you understand more about how the government actually works. At this point, you should at least be able to recognize how much of the news and newspaper headlines have to do with government — local, state, and federal. When you are 18 and old enough to vote, you will have a power granted to you by the Twenty-Sixth Amendment to the U.S. Constitution. But, by the time you finish this book, you should realize that even now you are a part of government and that your own involvement is the key to better government. ■

To find out more...
start with the *Governing Illinois* web site at **www.uis.edu/govern**

Case study:

Governments Working Together to Get Rid of Garbage (or Maybe Not)

By Darlene Emmert Fisher and James M. Banovetz

Some powers and duties are handled by only one government. The federal government, for instance, acts by itself when providing military force to defend this country or to assist other countries. The Illinois state government is the only form of government that provides regular government funding to operate this state's public universities. And only local governments — cities, villages, and special districts — provide services like ambulance squads.

But, solutions to most public problems involve different levels of government — national, state, and local — working together. For many routine services, such as providing social services to the poor, the different levels of government work together relatively smoothly. For instance, the national government sets up certain welfare services and provides money to the states so they can operate the programs. The states then set up rules telling who gets helped and how the money will be used. Local governments, in turn, deliver the social services to needy people in each community.

The relationship between the people who want and need government services and the many different levels of government is often very cordial. For example, most times people and governments find it relatively easy to work together to reduce crime. There can be a little bit of friction when it comes to improving schools (especially figuring out who pays for the improvements). But sometimes the relationships can get very awkward.

The Garbage Problem

Getting rid of garbage is a problem that attracts little public interest. But it is a big problem. Recent estimates are that Americans produce 209.7 tons of garbage a year. It has to go somewhere. Part of the solution is to put nonhazardous waste into landfills.

In 1997, the Illinois Environmental Protection Agency released its tenth annual *Landfill Capacity Report*. At the time, there were 57 active landfills in the state. Thanks to recycling, those landfills had had to absorb less garbage than in years past. But even so, the 1997 capacity report said that, if all things held constant, the state's landfills would be full in 10 years.

To be responsible citizens, we must look to our future needs. We can't ignore the problem for a decade and just let the trash pile up. Consider how many rats would thrive if garbage weren't disposed of properly. Imagine how the water supply could become contaminated. Imagine how sick people could get. Imagine the smell! So, to avoid running out of landfill space, some current landfills will have to increase their capacity and some new waste treatment facilities will have to be built.

But here's a problem. Many people don't want a garbage disposal site in their community; they all want it in someone else's neighborhood. And here's another problem: Sometimes the government agencies involved in solving problems (such as where to put a landfill) have special interests that interfere with one another.

This case study shows how lots of different agencies of the state and national government can get involved in the public's interest to solve the garbage dump dilemma. But sometimes these agencies each seek to protect a *different* public interest. Local residents have firm ideas about what they do and don't want — especially when the issue involves something as noxious as garbage. This puts government between a rock and a hard place. This case study illustrates how different government agencies, working both with and against each other at the same time, try to solve tough problems.

Local governments provide services such as garbage disposal.

Who Gets Involved in the Garbage Problem?

State law now requires that all counties and the city of Chicago develop waste management programs, including recycling. There is a tax on garbage hauled to landfills, and the proceeds from that tax help communities start recycling programs. But there is still a lot of garbage to be disposed of, and, as the Illinois Environmental Protection Agency reported, we are running out of places to put it.

Illinois state law also says new landfills can only be opened if local residents agree to them. But deciding where to put a landfill doesn't begin and end with a local government. The problem involves many different governments. Townships, especially in rural areas, often provide dumping facilities, but in doing so they must protect their residents and their land, water, and air from the pollution that landfills can create.

State government is also concerned with protection of the environment from dangerous waste. The Illinois Environmental Protection Agency has established standards for potential problem areas like landfills, trash dumps, and factory waste disposal. The Department of Nuclear Safety is concerned with the disposal of low level nuclear waste. The Illinois Geological Survey and Illinois Water Survey are concerned with landfill sites because of the effect that trash has on seepage in sand, earth, rock formations, and underground water supplies. Even the state park system must protect its parks from trash.

At the federal level, there is another Environmental Protection Agency that establishes national standards regarding tolerable amounts of environmental damage. Special legislation protects particular areas such as wetlands, which often seem to be wasteland to local observers and yet are important parts of the ecological system and are vital to sustaining forms of wildlife and controlling some flooding problems. The U.S. Army Corps of Engineers is charged with oversight of river and lake projects on the nation's waterways and has a responsibility to protect waterways from pollution.

Recycling is only one part of a waste management program.

What To Do With Trash in Northern Cook County?

Let's take the case of the Northwest Municipal Conference, an organization of 31 suburbs in northern Cook County. In the mid-1980s, the conference planned to take responsibility for all the waste produced by its member communities, so it proposed to set up a "balefill," a disposal area where compressed packages of waste would be deposited.

The conference chose a site in an isolated area in the village of Bartlett, west of Chicago, for the balefill, and it set up a new, special district unit of government called the Solid Waste Agency of Northern Cook County (SWANCC).

Opposition to the proposed location for the balefill came immediately from residents and communities in the vicinity of the suggested site,

The simple question of where can we throw our garbage can take years to answer. The answer must take into account the community's interest in protecting the purity of its drinking water, the interests of the landfill's neighbors in protecting their property values and preventing landscape littering and pollution, the concerns of those interested in the preservation of wildlife, and everyone who wants to reduce the cost of garbage disposal.

and from more distant communities concerned that the balefill would pollute underground drinking water supplies. Environmentalists were also concerned because the proposed site included one of the few remaining nesting sites for blue herons in the northern Illinois region. The Not in My Back Yard (or NIMBY) argument worked two ways. Communities close to the site objected to having the balefill near them; communities more distant were delighted to put the balefill in that site because then it would not be in their back yard.

In a situation like this, a small number of angry opponents may have a dramatic influence. Governmental boards, especially those at the local level, are accustomed to very limited citizen interest in their work. The very vocal and sometimes dramatic protests of even a small group of people may be very influential at these board meetings. Local officials, especially, do not like to be unpopular with their neighbors. Their reluctance to act on even urgent problems in the face of NIMBY opposition has led to another phenomenon, "NIMTO" (Not In My Term of Office), in which problems are simply postponed by government officials because no one wants to deal with them. When politicians can't put off a decision, they work especially hard to appease organized constituent groups.

The Decision Process

Once the SWANCC decided to proceed with its balefill plan, the proposal went to the Cook County government for zoning approval. Despite strong protests from officials in adjacent communities and from citizens groups, the Cook County Board gave preliminary approval to the plan, but only after developing a way to establish a one million dollar per year fund to guarantee the value of neighboring property and the safety of drinking water supplies.

Opposition then focused on the next step: the required approval from the Illinois Environmental Protection Agency. That agency originally found problems with groundwater monitoring at the site. Groundwater is important because the old gravel pit site of the balefill could potentially leak into an underground water supply from which many communities pump their drinking water. After changes in the plans were made to further protect the groundwater supplies, the Illinois EPA did approve the balefill.

Next, the approval process went to the U.S. Army Corps of Engineers. Since the proposed site fills with storm water runoff part of the year and serves as a habitat for migratory waterfowl, it came under the corps' jurisdiction.

The problem was immediately complicated for the corps by a U.S. congressman who opposed the balefill. He added an amendment to a congressional appropriations bill for funding the corps: The amendment would require the corps to consult with the U.S. Environmental Protection Agency and report to Congress about potential water problems.

Routine procedures require that the corps hold a public hearing on the issue and solicit input from other affected government agencies. Among those that provided such input were the Illinois Department of Conservation, the Illinois Endangered Species Board, the U.S. Department of the Interior, the U.S. Environmental Protection Agency, and the federal agency concerned with migratory fowl and wildlife. Most recommended against building the proposed balefill site.

In January 1991, the corps denied the permit on the grounds that the analysis of alternative sites was not complete and the impact on wildlife was unacceptable. SWANCC (the special district set up to deal with the landfill issue) promptly revised its alternative site study, revised its wildlife assistance plan and resubmitted the plan to the corps. On July 21, 1994, the corps denied the permit application for the second time. This time the basis for the denial was much more broad than the earlier decision. The corps gave five reasons for its refusal:

1. Not enough analysis of alternatives.
2. The area could not be properly made into a landfill habitat.
3. Another location might be a useful alternative.
4. SWANCC did not prove it could maintain the area for the long term.
5. SWANCC didn't prove that composting was not a possible alternative.

At this point SWANCC found itself facing a common problem in the field of government. Before it could develop the landfill, it had to get approvals from lots of different people, and that is a tough job. SWANCC couldn't get the OK from the U.S. Army Corps of Engineers, an agency that was acting in response to a number of groups and motivated by its own mission to protect the usability of the nation's water supplies. The landfill problem was now stuck.

So, SWANCC turned to the court system. It sued the U.S. Army Corps of Engineers. SWANCC asked the district court to:

1. Rule that the corps lacked jurisdiction in the matter (that is, that the corps didn't have the authority to block the project), and
2. Look over the corps' interpretation of the facts in the case to determine that the corps made an incorrect decision.

The district court ruled that the U.S. Army Corps of Engineers did indeed have jurisdiction in the matter. In 1998, SWANCC withdrew its request for the district court to review the corps' interpretation of the facts. SWANCC decided instead to appeal the district court's holding that the corps had proper jurisdiction in the matter to the U.S. court of appeals.

As of the publication of this book in 1999, SWANCC was still waiting for the U.S. court of appeals. Questions from a landfill placement process that started in the mid-1980s remained unresolved so many years later.

How the Case Illustrates Three Elements of Government Interaction

Three elements are important to note from this description of a real case of intergovernmental relations.

First, the business of government is very complex. Even a simple question — where do I throw my garbage — is a hard question that can take years to answer. The answer must take into account not only your interest in getting rid of your garbage, but the community's interest in protecting the purity of its drinking water, the interests of the landfill's neighbors in protecting their property values and preventing landscape littering and pollution, the concerns of those interested in the preservation of wildlife, and everyone who is concerned with keeping down the cost of garbage disposal.

Second, there are a number of different government agencies and governments involved in providing services to the public. For example, this case involves 31 suburbs that are members of the Northwest Municipal Conference; 23 suburbs that formed the special district (SWANCC); the municipalities that did not join; Cook County government; several dif-

For More Information

Keep on the Case

When *Governing Illinois* went to press in 1999, SWANCC was still awaiting a ruling from the U.S. district court of appeals to determine whether or not the U.S. Army Corps of Engineers had jurisdiction in the matter of where to put the landfill. For updates, please check the *Governing Illinois* web site at www.uis.edu/govern. ■

CASE STUDY
SUM IT UP

This case is an illustration of what happens when everyone agrees there is a problem, but no one agrees on how to solve it. The resulting dilemma is typical of the problem solving difficulties that are the everyday work of government.

There are no heroes or villains in this case. None of the decision-makers stands to make money from any particular outcome. No one has a personal stake in the outcome. But they all agree there is a problem — where to dispose of the region's garbage — and all are genuinely trying to solve the problem in the manner that will best serve the public interest.

The people involved in this case have been working a long time — more than ten years — and, as of the time of this book's publication, the issue is still not resolved. Why? Because different people have different ideas about how best to serve the public. So, the solution needs much study, involves many people, and requires numerous compromises.

Different governments or government agencies speak for the legitimate concerns of different people. SWANCC speaks for those looking for a place to dump their garbage. The Village of Bartlett speaks for those whose homes are near the site of the proposed dump. State and federal environmental agencies are concerned about matters such as water quality, bird life, and public health. The U.S. Army Corps of Engineers is charged by Congress with protecting the nation's water resources. All are being given a say in the outcome of this matter. It takes a long time for so many voices to be heard and for so many opinions to be weighed against one another. ■

To find out more...
start with the *Governing Illinois* web site at **www.uis.edu/govern**

ferent agencies of the state of Illinois; several different agencies of the federal government; and even the U.S. Congress. All of these governmental units have a part of the answer to the simple question, "Where can I throw my garbage?"

Third, each of the different agencies is not just an added layer of bureaucratic red tape, but a source for new ideas about how to prevent the landfill from harming anything or anyone. The Northwest Municipal Conference offered many suggestions to make the landfill an acceptable neighbor. The new, special district, SWANCC, was created. The opposition of other communities and groups led SWANCC and other government agencies to look harder for answers to their concerns. As a result, SWANCC set up the fund to protect property values and drinking water; the Illinois EPA forced improvements in the groundwater monitoring system and built in more safety measures; and the U.S. Army Corps of Engineers called for SWANCC to consider using another site as a practicable alternative.

Even though the matter has ended up in court, the input of each different government agency is helping to determine a solution that may ultimately protect the environment at this location while promoting a solid waste transportation technology that could serve SWANCC for decades. ■

Chapter 3

The Constitution of the State of Illinois is more than just a document to be warehoused in the Illinois State Library. It represents an evolving, ongoing contract between the people of Illinois and their government.

Constitutionalism: A Contract with the People

by Denny L. Schillings

Illinois state government and our national government have many things in common. Their constitutions are similar insofar as they establish a system of government, affirm citizen rights, and impose limitations on government. Both governments are democratic republics. They are republican in form because their decisions are made by officials elected by their

Federalism A system of government in which power is divided between a central authority and constituent political units, known as states in the U.S. system.

Article An individual section of the U.S. Constitution. The Constitution of the State of Illinois is also divided into articles.

Expressed powers Powers specifically mentioned in the U.S. Constitution and given to either the federal or state government.

Implied powers Powers not listed in the U.S. Constitution but powers that are determined to be needed by the federal government in order for it to be able to govern effectively.

Reserved powers Powers that the U.S. Constitution neither delegates to the federal government nor prohibits the states from exercising.

citizens. At the same time they are democratic governments because there are regular elections with decisions determined by majority vote, and the powers of the governments are ultimately vested in the people.

We are a nation of fifty state governments operating simultaneously with the national government in Washington, D.C. The only way it can work successfully is through cooperation. The document that establishes that cooperation is the U.S. Constitution.

When delegates from each state met in Philadelphia in the summer of 1787 to write a constitution for the nation, they faced a monumental problem: how to balance powers of individual states and powers of a central government serving the entire nation. Each of the states was worried about the loss of power to a centralized government with too much authority. The first attempt at a national government under the Articles of Confederation did not work very well for the United States of America. Our young nation lacked a strong central government, and the individual states were not cooperating with one another. The delegates in Philadelphia agreed that they had to craft a constitution to insure cooperation of states as a nation, and, at the same time, protect the interests of the individual states.

The Concept of Federalism

Like most decisions made by the delegates, the problem of states' rights was dealt with through a series of compromises. The United States Constitution divides authority, giving the national government certain specific powers, reserving to the states other powers, and establishing that some authority is shared between the state and national governments. This system of government is called federalism.

While **federalism** explains the relationship of the states to the national government, it is a concept that can help in understanding the relationship between a state government and all its local governments. The Illinois Constitution establishes the central state government and the framework for local governments throughout the state. Basic local governments in Illinois include the county and city or village. There are also townships within counties. Other local governments have special purposes and include school districts and many other types, from library to airport districts. Before you tackle local governments, you first need to understand the relationship of powers between the national and state governments.

The government isn't always some remote concept. Government can be your neighbors. The District 303 Board of Education serving the Pekin area is a special-purpose local government.

Federalism in the United States Constitution

The powers of the national government, in relation to the states, are outlined in the **articles** of the U.S. Constitution. Certain powers are **expressed**, meaning they are directly mentioned in the Constitution. Most of the expressed powers of the national government are listed in the first three articles of the Constitution. Among the expressed powers are such things as making treaties, coining money, raising and maintaining an army, declaring war, and carrying on relations with foreign governments.

Another type of power is **implied** in the Constitution, meaning that these powers are necessary to govern but are not listed in the Constitution. In order to raise an army, for example, the government has sometimes used a draft, which requires eligible citizens to serve in the military. Although not specified in the Constitution, a draft was found necessary for raising an army in times of crisis. The U.S. Congress passed a bill establishing a draft, the president signed the bill into law, and the U.S. Supreme Court decided that the power was allowed by the U.S. Constitution. (Today, all men, at age eighteen, must register with the U.S. Selective Service for a possible draft into military service.)

In order for the national government to do things that are necessary but not listed in the Constitution, it relies on Article I, Section 8. It gives the national government the ability to "make all Laws which shall be necessary and proper" to carry out its duties under the Constitution. Like a rubber band, this "elastic clause" allows government to expand or contract its authority.

One example of expanding and contracting national authority occurred in the 1970s when an oil shortage threatened the nation. Congress, in an attempt to conserve oil, passed a 55 miles per hour speed limit law for the nation. At the time, state highways generally had speed limits of 65 or 70 miles, per hour. The Illinois General Assembly, like many other state legislatures, did not feel the lower speed limit was necessary and refused to adopt it. In order to enforce the 55 miles per hour speed limit, Congress said federal money for state highways would not be sent to a state unless the state complied with the national speed limit. In need of such money to maintain highways, Illinois reluctantly accepted the limit imposed by Congress. In this case, the ability of the national government to dictate to the states seemed necessary.

The Constitution is flexible though, and what one Congress creates, another can change or repeal. By 1995, oil shortages were a thing of the past, more efficient automobile engines used less gasoline and oil production was increasing. In response, Congress repealed the federal speed limit and returned speed regulation to the states. Illinois' response to the new authority was to maintain the 55 limit in urban areas and on two-lane highways and increase the speed limit to 65 on noncongested four-lane or interstate routes.

The framers of the U.S. Constitution were skeptical of the authority of the strong national government they were creating, and they placed certain limitations on it. In Article I, Section 9, they specifically denied certain powers to the national government.

Still fearful that individual rights of citizens might be abused by the national government, ten amendments were added soon after the adoption of the U.S. Constitution. They are called the Bill of Rights. Nine of the ten protect specific rights of citizens, and the Tenth Amendment protects the states' **reserved powers**. The Tenth Amendment says: "The powers not delegated to the United States by the Constitution, nor prohibited by it to the States, are reserved

The Constitution is flexible. What one Congress creates, another can change: In the 1970s, in an attempt to conserve oil during an oil shortage, Congress passed a 55 miles per hour speed limit law for the nation. But by 1995, oil shortages were a thing of the past. In response, Congress repealed the federal speed limit and returned speed regulation to the states.

Concurrent powers Powers shared by the national and state governments.

to the States respectively, or to the people."

As a result, states can exercise any power not given to the national government nor denied to them by the Constitution. For example, Illinois can establish a public school system, regulate licenses for driving, and set age limits to purchase alcohol.

Just as they were fearful of an overly powerful national government, the framers of the U.S. Constitution saw the need to restrict state authority as well. Article I, Section 10 lists the powers denied to the states. Specifically the states cannot make treaties, coin money, tax imports and exports, or declare war.

You can see that federalism works by defining both the authority and limitations of the national and state governments' powers. There is yet another set of powers in federalism: **Concurrent powers** are shared by the national and state governments, meaning they use them at the same time. A good example is the power to tax. In Illinois, citizens who smoke pay a federal cigarette tax, a state cigarette tax, and, in some cases, a city cigarette tax. Each level of government sets the amount of tax and decides how the tax money will be used. As long as a power is not specifically reserved to either the state or national government, it may be shared. The ability to share power is one of the most important aspects of federalism. By sharing certain powers, governments at the different levels can each deal with a similar problem, but in different ways. For example, smoking is a health hazard. The national government has banned smoking in airplanes it regulates. Illinois state government has passed laws assuring there is no smoking in most public buildings in the state. Both governments have acted to protect the health of citizens.

What happens if a conflict arises over which level of government has a certain power? Article VI of the U.S. Constitution states:

> This Constitution, and the Laws of the United States which shall be made in pursuance thereof; and all Treaties made, or which shall be made, under the Authority of the United States, shall be the supreme Law of the Land; and the Judges in every State shall be bound thereby, any Thing in the Constitution or Laws or any State to the Contrary notwithstanding.

This is the "supremacy clause" that restricts state laws and state constitutions from conflicting with the U.S. Constitution and laws. Since the U.S. Constitution and laws are supreme, state officials are expected to follow them. Local governments, such as cities and counties, which get their authority from the state, cannot pass laws conflicting with the U.S. Constitution and federal laws or with the Constitution of the State of Illinois and state laws.

Rights and Responsibilities of the Federal System

The idea of shared power works only when both the national and state governments fulfill their responsibilities to each other. For example, the U.S. Constitution guarantees to each state a republican form of government. This means that the national government must assure the citizens in each state that their state government will be directed by persons who are elected by the voters of that state.

The national government of our United States of America also has responsibility for protecting states against invasion and domestic violence. At times during our history, the national government has been asked to restore calm within a state. During railroad rioting in Chicago in 1877 and the early 1880s, for example, federal troops were called in to restore peace.

The national government must also respect the geographic boundaries of each state. Article IV, Section 3 of the U.S. Constitution clearly explains that "no new State shall be formed or erected within the Jurisdiction of any other State ... without the Consent of the Legislatures."

Beyond the expectation to cooperate with the national government, states also have specific responsibilities. All elections for national government officials — the president, the vice president, U.S. senators, and U.S. representatives — are carried out by the states. The dates for the national general elections are set by national law, but the state sets the hours, place, and manner in which all elections are carried out.

Understanding that the Constitution might need to be altered by future events, its framers allowed for a method of amendment. The states play an important part in the amending process. No amendment to the U.S. Constitution can take effect unless three-fourths of the states approve it. While a single state's acceptance or rejection of a proposed amendment would seem to be a relatively minor action, it can be of great importance. An example is the proposed Equal Rights Amendment (guaranteeing women and men equal rights as citizens), which was submitted to the states for ratification about twenty-five years ago. By 1977, only thirty-five of a necessary thirty-seven states had approved the proposed amendment, and it failed to become part of the U.S. Constitution. Illinois, whose Constitution grants equal protection of individual rights to men and women in its own Bill of Rights, was one of the states that did not ratify the amendment.

At the time, most political analysts felt that if Illinois were to ratify the amendment, other states would follow. However, the Equal Rights Amendment did not get enough votes to pass in the Illinois General Assembly. For Illinois to ratify an amendment, both the Illinois House and Illinois Senate must approve it.

One successful example of the states' power to change the U.S. Constitution took place in July 1971, when the Twenty-Sixth Amendment gave eighteen-year-olds the right to vote. Prior to this amendment, most states, including Illinois, required citizens to be at least twenty-one years of age to be qualified to vote. Pressure came for the change from citizens. The national government was sending U.S. military forces to fight in Vietnam, and the argument was that if military service began at age eighteen, so should the right to vote. In 1970, Congress lowered the voting age, but the U.S. Supreme Court ruled that Congress did not have the power to set voting age qualifications for elections, that it was a state power according to the U.S. Constitution. Congress has the power to propose constitutional amendments, so it proposed one to give all eighteen-year-olds the right to vote. The required number of states quickly ratified it, including Illinois, by votes in the General Assembly. The amendment process is one reason the Constitution is known as a living document.

Reciprocity The concept of mutual cooperation or exchange of privilege that allows citizens of one state to function easily in other states.

Extradition Surrender of a fugitive to the jurisdiction of another state.

Relations Between the States

While the basis for our U.S. Constitution is the cooperation between the states and the national government, relations between and among the states are also important. They must cooperate with and respect one another. States did not cooperate under the old Articles of Confederation. Contracts or legal notices made in one state were ignored in another. State borders, especially those along rivers, were a constant source of conflict. States were generally jealous or envious of others. The people in the small states with less land and smaller populations felt threatened by large ones, and large states often ignored small states. Wealthy states were envied by poor states. Even states of comparable size and wealth were hostile to each other. Competition among the states was strong. It still is.

With such a background, the framers of the U.S. Constitution carefully approached the question of interstate relations. Their answer is in Article IV: Each state is to honor the actions of the other states, respecting court decisions, laws, and various licenses. Today, each state accepts most legal documents of the others. For example, a driver's license from Illinois allows the holder to drive legally when in other states. This concept of mutual cooperation, known as **reciprocity**, allows citizens of one state to function easily in other states.

The concept of reciprocity allows out-of-staters the right to buy fishing licenses so that Illinois' water resources, such as the Rock River, can be opened up to sportspersons from every state.

Article IV also expects each state to give citizens of the other states the same rights as its own citizens. There are some exceptions allowed by the U.S. Supreme Court. For example, as an Illinois citizen you may attend a state-funded university, go to a state-owned park, or get a state fishing license. Someone from Indiana or Florida cannot be barred from any of those Illinois public places or from getting a state license, but as out-of-state residents they can be charged more than Illinois residents.

Each state's law applies to anyone living in or visiting the state. Assume that selling fireworks is legal in Indiana. In Illinois, the state legislature has outlawed the sale of fireworks without proper licenses, and then certain types of fireworks can only be sold to people who have proper permits. Let's say an Illinois resident drives to Indiana and buys a trunkload of fireworks. Can he or she, as a resident of Illinois, legally buy these fireworks? Yes, because while in Indiana he or she was under Indiana law (which we will assume allows the sale). What if the same individual brought the fireworks back to Illinois, didn't get the necessary licenses, and sold the fireworks? Can he or she legally sell them in Illinois since they were bought legally in Indiana? No, because the Illinois law governs his actions when they take place in Illinois. The application of individual state laws within their own borders is a part of the idea of Article IV, which says that states must respect each other's laws.

Extradition of criminals is another understanding between the states. If a person charged with a crime in Illinois flees to Michigan, he or she is supposed to be returned to Illinois by Michigan to stand trial under Illinois law. The U.S. Constitution gives each state's governor the responsibility for abiding by extradition agreements. The governor does have the option of refusing the extradition of someone to another state, but most states willingly cooperate with one another in criminal matters.

Illinois' State Constitution

While the U.S. Constitution is supreme in our nation, each state has its own constitution setting out the powers and organization of its state government. Before Illinois could become a state, it had to adopt a constitution. That was in 1818; since then, Illinois has adopted a new constitution three different times: in 1848, 1870, and 1970. The present Constitution was drafted in a constitutional convention held in 1969 and 1970 and ratified by the state's voters in December 1970.

Although four state constitutions may seem like a lot, because there has been only a single U.S. Constitution, it is not uncommon for states to have several. Since the U.S. Constitution is written in broad terms, the need to amend seldom occurs. State constitutions, however, tend to deal with more specific activities and are subject to changing conditions. The 1818 Constitution of the State of Illinois, for example, was written to accommodate the needs of a frontier state with a limited population. By 1848, Illinois' population had grown, demand for services was increasing, a larger court system was necessary. A general overhaul of the legislature was needed to work with emerging local governments. The 1848 Constitution, which was three times longer than the one adopted in 1818, addressed many of these concerns and established the structure of government we have today.

The Constitutions of 1870 and 1970 further refined the 1848 work and sought to bring state government in line with changing population base, industrial practices, and political realities in the state. Although there is no current movement to create a new state constitution, it is possible that someday yet another version will emerge to address needs of governing at that time.

The Constitution of the State of Illinois adopted in 1970 is much like the U.S. Constitution. It contains a Bill of Rights and separate articles that provide for a legislative branch (called the Illinois General Assembly), an executive branch (headed by the governor as the state's chief executive officer), and a judicial branch with three levels of state courts (headed by the Illinois Supreme Court). The Illinois Constitution also establishes the state's local government and public education systems.

Most government services are, in fact, delivered to citizens by the state or local government, not by the national government. It is state government that has the primary responsibility for education, public safety, health and welfare, and the regulation of business and the professions. While it is true that the national government may pass laws and provide some money for all these services, it is the state government that figures out how to deliver these services to its citizens. It is also the state government that figures out how to get much of the money to finance the services that citizens expect.

Education is a State Responsibility

Education is one such area of state responsibility. It's different in other nations. In some Western European countries, students in a particular grade study the same subject matter, at the same time, throughout the entire country. Requirements for graduation are exactly the same in every school of the nation: To receive a diploma, students must pass a standardized test. Unlike these nations, the United States does not have a national policy for education. In fact, the U.S. Constitution does not deal with education at all.

Article X of the Illinois Constitution establishes responsibility for education. Section 1 says:

A fundamental goal of the People of the State is the educational development of all persons to the limits of their capacities.

The State shall provide for an efficient system of high quality public educational institutions and services. Education in public schools through the secondary level shall be free. There may be such other free education as the General Assembly provides by law.

The State has the primary responsibility for financing the system, of public education.

In order to oversee the state's educational system, the Illinois Constitution created a State Board of Education. The board is responsible for establishing general goals, evaluating programs, and suggesting ways to finance schools.

Education is a good example of how the federalism concept of shared responsibility extends through the state to the local level. The actual responsibility for education has been passed on by the state to local school districts. In 1998, Illinois had 898 public school districts. While the state legislature passes laws affecting all the districts and the State Board of Education does much planning, each local district elects a board to set local school policy and control the budget. There are exceptions, notably Chicago, where the city has taken control of schools. Under school reform legislation enacted in 1989 by the General Assembly, however, every Chicago school (all 485 of them) has an elected

The responsibility for education has been passed on by the state to local school districts.

Public safety is a responsibility shared by the federal and state governments. Here, the Illinois National Guard erects a wall of sandbags to prevent flood damage.

local school council — consisting of six parent representatives; two community representatives; two teachers; one principal; and one student representative in each high school — to administer its school. There is still an overall central administrative office run by a Chief Executive Officer (a CEO), but the school councils have been granted specific powers to control their own schools.

Despite the constitutional promise that the state has the primary responsibility for financing the system of public education, local property taxpayers in many school districts provide the majority of funds to operate their schools. Some districts are poorer than others, however. The result of this imbalance in funding is a wide difference from district to district in the money spent to teach each student. Paying taxes for your education in Illinois is an issue today. In 1997 a proposal to guarantee a base finding level starting at $4,225 for every pupil passed, but not without controversy. If the state is to give more money to the less wealthy districts, it might have to increase taxes. But state taxes are paid by everyone in Illinois, and taxpayers in the wealthy districts might complain because their districts would not get any more money from the state. Money is often the issue in government. Few citizens want to pay more taxes, but at the same time many want government to spend more money on "good" things like education.

Public Safety is a Shared Responsibility

Public safety is another area of shared government authority. The U.S. Constitution gives Congress the power to maintain military forces to protect the nation. State government is, in turn, given the right to have a militia (called a national guard) to keep peace and enforce its laws. The National Guard is seldom used except in emergencies. The Guard may be called out if there is a bad flood or earthquake damage; it may be called out to control riots, such as during the 1968 Democratic National Convention in Chicago. It may also be called into active service by the president as part of the national armed services as in Operation Desert Shield and Desert Storm in the Persian Gulf in 1990, and it may be placed on alert in times of crisis.

In the Preamble of the Illinois Constitution, Illinois government is given the responsibility of providing for the "safety and welfare" of the people. The state government's direct response to this duty is a rather limited one. The Illinois State Police have only about 1,700 officers patrolling the highways, investigating certain violations of the law, and providing protection for state officials. In addition, the State Police provide assistance to local authorities through the state crime lab and other specialized services.

As in education, the majority of police are under the control of local governments. Each of the 102 counties in the state has a sheriff's department. Within those counties nearly 1,300 cities, villages, and towns have police departments ranging in size from Chicago with 13,500 officers to small towns with only one. Every level of government shares equally the responsibility for the safety of citizens.

Health and Welfare Responsibilities

Another area where the state expands on the national government's responsibility is in health and welfare. Illinois has state agencies to inspect food, monitor diseases, and license physicians and nurses. The mentally ill are treated in state hospitals or provided care in their communities with state financial support. State agencies provide services for families and children, specifically protecting children from child abuse and granting to poorer citizens both welfare payments and health services. Other state departments assist in helping people with alcohol and drug problems and in rehabilitation of disabled people.

The growing national concern over the environment is also a state and local issue. The Illinois Constitution makes the provision and maintenance of a healthful environment the public policy of the state and the duty of each person. The Illinois Environmental Protection Agency and the Illinois Pollution Control Board see that state environmental laws are obeyed. Air and water quality, radiation control, garbage and sewage disposal, and hazardous waste management are only a few of the areas regulated by state laws. There are also federal environmental laws that the state and its residents must obey.

As might be expected when responsibility is shared, there are disagreements between governments. When the national government approached the state for permission to deposit hazardous solid waste material in abandoned mines in south-

An Illinois Environmental Protection Agency scientist takes water samples to check for bio-contaminants.

Regulation of business and working conditions has fallen onto the shoulders of state governments.

ern and central Illinois, the Illinois legislature gave tentative approval. Several possible sites were selected. Then, as more information was released on the type and hazards of the waste material, many citizens did not like the idea and the state reconsidered. It rejected the proposal. This is a good example of how state government can exercise its rights over the national government.

Business Regulation by State Government

Regulation of business has also fallen onto the shoulders of state governments. The U.S. Constitution gave Congress the power to regulate commerce among the states. This so-called "commerce clause" of the Constitution has been used by Congress to regulate television and radio stations, airlines, railroads, and other industries doing business in different states. But, for the most part, businesses operating within the borders of Illinois are regulated by state laws.

Public utility companies such as Commonwealth Edison, Northern Illinois Gas, or Illinois Power are subject to the regulations imposed by state law. Insurance companies, real estate agencies, and even funeral homes are governed by rules established by the state. Working conditions are also affected by the state. The safety and sanitary conditions of our factories, as well as the number of hours an employee may work, are established by the state. The state oversees the unemployment insurance program for workers who lose their jobs in Illinois and the workers' compensation program for workers who get hurt on the job.

Local Government in Illinois

Yet another level of shared responsibility exists between Illinois state government and local governments within the state. However, the 102 county governments, the 1,300 city and village governments, and the 5,000-plus local government agencies are not partners with the state in the same

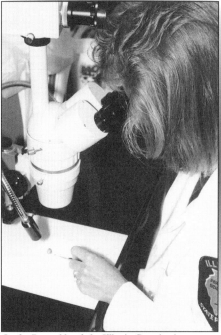

In the Preamble of the Illinois Constitution, Illinois government is given the responsibility of providing for the "safety and welfare" of the people. The state government's direct response to this mandate has been to form the Illinois State Police, who provide assistance to local authorities through the state crime lab and other specialized services.

SUM IT UP

In the United States, our system of government has many levels, with a system of government in which power is divided between a central authority, as outlined in the U.S. Constitution, and the various states. This form of government, called federalism, allows money, power, rights, and responsibilities to flow both from and to each of the governmental bodies, yet retains the concept of democracy.

The similarities between the U.S. Constitution and the Illinois Constitution are striking, beginning in each document with the words "We the people...". In both documents it is the people that government is meant to represent. The concept of federalism, shared power, from the national through the state to the local level, allows the people a clear and direct voice in deciding their own affairs through their elected representatives. As you continue to study the Illinois Constitution, remember that each level of government is a link in the chain that allows our system to be, in Abraham Lincoln's words, a "government of the people, by the people, for the people". ■

To find out more...
start with the *Governing Illinois* web site at **www.uis.edu/govern**

sense as the state is with the national government. Local governments generally have only the powers granted them by state statutes, but there is an exception.

Article VII of the 1970 Constitution of the State of Illinois gives **home rule** to some local governments. Home rule means that local governments can, within limits, determine their own powers. To try something new, home-rule governments do not have to get a state law enacted like the rest of the local governments. According to Article VII, all cities and villages with populations over 25,000 have home rule. If a smaller city or village wants home rule, their voters can approve it by referendum. Voters can also take away home rule by referendum. As of 1999, over 140 Illinois cities and villages had home rule.

County governments can also have home rule, but the power and structure of the county government — not population — is the factor that determines whether a county government is eligible for home rule. Only Cook County, the most populous, has had home rule since the 1970 Illinois Constitution was adopted.

No other type of local government in Illinois can have home rule.

So most of Illinois' counties, cities, and villages and all of its townships, school districts, airport authorities, library districts, and other local governments with special services depend on state laws for their powers.

Illinois local governments often overlap in their boundaries and in their services to the public. What they have in common is that decisions are made by boards representing the citizens within the boundaries and taxes are levied within the boundaries to fund the local government services.

Chapters 7 and 8 provide greater detail on local government and taxes. But, for now, it is useful to keep in mind that Illinois local government finances itself, much like the state and nation, by taxing its residents. Unlike the state and federal government which, for the most part, tax income, local governments in Illinois tax property. Homeowners, farm owners, and business owners pay taxes on their residences, buildings, and lands. Property taxes account for well over half of the money available to local governments. But Illinois state government shares some of the state income tax and sales tax money with all the counties, cities, and villages in Illinois. It gives other money to local governments, too, such as schools. The state receives money from the national government, too, for example, to build major highways and fund welfare programs.

The different levels of government could not function without the concurrent ability to tax and spend money, independent from the other levels, but local governments depend on some money from the state government, and the state government depends on some money from the national government.

While the local government has greater independence under home rule, it also has specific limitations on taxing powers set by the Illinois Constitution. A home-rule government cannot pass a local income tax, unless the Illinois state legislature decides to give this authority to all the municipalities and counties in the state. ■

Chapter 4

The Illinois Senate in session

The Legislative Game: How to Pass Your Law

by Judy Lee (Lewis) Uphoff

If you want a law passed in Illinois, there is only one way to do that: You must become a player in the legislative game. The game is played every year from the second Wednesday in January until May or June in the Capitol in Springfield, Illinois. That's when the Illinois General Assembly is in session. The chief players are, of course, the 177 legislators elected by the people in their districts. These legislators are the members of the Illinois

General Assembly, which forms the **legislative branch** of Illinois' state government. (See "Electing 118 House Members, 59 Senate Members.")

The main duty or function of the legislative branch is to make or enact laws — or prevent the enactment of laws — for the people of the state. The legislative branch is divided into two houses, the **Illinois House of Representatives** and the **Illinois Senate**. Illinois has patterned its government after the federal government, and has two chambers (or houses) in the legislative branch. No bill can become a law unless it passes both houses of the legislative branch with exactly the same wording. This arrangement makes passing legislation more difficult than if there were only one chamber. This is exactly the idea: To protect the people of the state from useless or even dangerous legislation, two houses must agree that the bill should become a law.

All of the above may sound a little complicated, and you may think that, just because you are only a student and not a legislator, there is no way for you to play or even have any part in the legislative game. However, you, too, can play the game with a chance of passing the legislation that you wish to see enacted.

Electing 118 House members, 59 Senate members

All information concerning the legislative branch can be found in Article IV of the Illinois Constitution. In Section 2 of Article IV the Constitution defines the makeup of the General Assembly.

After each U. S. census, the state has to be redivided into 59 legislative districts, thus 59 Illinois senators.

• One-third of the districts have their senators chosen for a four-year term, another four-year term, and then a two-year term.

• One-third will serve a four-year term, a two-year term, and a four-year term.

• The third group will serve a two-year term and then two four-year terms.

This term setup works out so that every ten years all senators are up for reelection following the census and the redrawing of the districts. Each district is supposed to be equal in population.

Each legislative district that elects one senator is divided into two representative districts, thus 118 members in the House. One representative is elected from each district and serves a two-year term.

To be either a senator or a representative you must be a U.S. citizen, twenty-one years old, and live in the district for two years prior to the election. You must also win the election in your district. Members are elected in even-numbered years. With the election in November, the House and Senate convene the following January. When they meet, the House of Representatives elects a speaker of the House, and the Senate elects a president of the Senate. The House and Senate also adopt detailed rules on how they will do their business. ■

Playing the Legislative Game

The basic rules are fairly easy, but, as in most games, it often takes more than just knowing the rules to win. It takes strategy, too.

Legislators can easily learn the basic rules of how a bill becomes a law, but they will not get bills enacted if they use the wrong strategy. Sometimes there are difficult decisions that make the game very hard to play — and win. Legislators must often make deals with other legislators to get support for their bills. Some bills may favor one part of the state over another, becoming a Chicago-versus-downstate issue.

Others might be good for the environment but cost businesses extra money. Sometimes legislators must decide between what they personally believe and what their **constituents** feel is important. They sometimes must decide between loyalty to their political party leaders and what they think is best.

The Players and Object of the Game

But let's get on with the game so you will understand how it works. To play the game, you must pick the playing piece you wish to use. You have four choices: Citizen, Lobbyist, Party Leader, and Governor. The object of the game is to convince the General Assembly to pass your bill. This is a complicated game involving a process that gives each legislator a vote and requires a **majority** vote to move a bill forward at each step.

Citizens

A citizen is anyone living in Illinois who thinks that some state law needs to be passed or changed. A citizen may be any age and have any kind of background. Usually he or she has found other citizens who believe that the same law needs to be passed or changed.

Lobbyists

A **lobbyist** is a person who is hired by some group to help get bills passed or defeated. Many of your parents may belong to groups that lobby. There are labor unions such as the United Auto Workers (UAW) and Illinois Educational Association (IEA); professional and business organizations, such as the American Medical Association (AMA), Illinois State Chamber of Commerce, Illinois Realtors, and the Illinois Farm Bureau; and other special interest organizations such as the National Rifle Association (NRA). These and many other groups hire lobbyists to influence legislators to vote for bills that would be beneficial to their group — or to vote against bills that would hurt their interests.

Party Leaders

Party leaders are influential members of the Democratic or Republican parties. They also try to decide what bills need to be passed. They encourage the legislators who belong to their party to introduce and pass bills that they feel are important. They also try to get individ-

Legislative branch One of three branches of Illinois state government. This branch is charged with creating state laws.

Illinois House of Representatives One of the two houses that make up the Illinois General Assembly, which is the state's lawmaking body. The House has 118 members, each elected from one of the state's 118 House districts.

Illinois Senate One of the two houses that make up the Illinois General Assembly, which is the state's lawmaking body. The Senate has 59 members, each elected from one of the state's 59 Senate districts.

Constituents The people who an elected official represents.

Majority A group or party who controls or wins more than half the votes of a legislative body.

Lobbyist Someone who tries to influence legislators to vote on issues the way a special interest group wants them to. Special interest groups can hire professional lobbyists, who, in Illinois, must register with the secretary of state.

Democrat Emil Jones of Chicago (above) was the Senate minority leader of the 91st Illinois General Assembly, while Republican Lee Daniels of Elmhurst was the House minority leader.

Minority A group or party that does not control or cannot win more than half the votes of a legislative body.

Minority leaders The highest ranking members of the political party that is in the minority in a unit of government. In Illinois there are minority leaders in both the House and Senate.

Majority leaders The highest ranking members of the political party that is in the majority in a unit of government. In Illinois there are majority leaders in both the House and Senate. In the Senate, the majority leader is the Senate president. In the House, the highest ranking majority leader is the speaker of the House, while the second-highest ranking member is usually given the title of majority leader.

Speaker of the House The highest ranking member of the majority party in the House.

Citizen initiative The ability of citizens to directly make legislation. The Constitution of the State of Illinois does not provide a way for citizens to introduce legislation to the General Assembly: They must do so indirectly by finding a state representative or a state senator to introduce a bill for them. Citizens may, however, bypass the General Assembly to amend the State Constitution.

Referendum An election in which voters decide an issue of public policy.

ual legislators from their party to take positions on issues that will help the party win the next election.

The term "party leadership" in the General Assembly includes the leaders of both the Democrats and the Republicans in both the Senate and the House. That means there are four top party leaders in the legislature. There are also very influential party leaders outside the General Assembly, such as the governor, the mayor of Chicago, or local party leaders who can influence legislators.

Which party has more power? The one with a majority of members, obviously, because it has the votes to approve bills. But one party may be the majority in the House, and the other may have the majority in the Senate. Whichever party has less than a majority of members is called the **minority** party. Both the House and Senate have **minority leaders**.

The **majority leader** in the Senate is the Senate president. The majority leader in the House is a separate position almost always held by a representative of the same party as the **speaker of the House**. The Senate president presides over meetings of the Senate, and the speaker of the House presides over those meetings of the House. They decide when bills will come up for debate and vote in their respective chambers. While the House speaker may not be officially called the majority leader, the speaker is considered by most to be the leader of his or her party's members in the House.

The leaders are very powerful in the Illinois General Assembly. As the leaders of their parties, they help members of their party get elected to office, appoint them to committees and leadership positions in the legislature, hire partisan staff, and direct their party's work in legislative sessions. They can and do have a strong influence on how individual members of the General Assembly vote on bills.

Many people feel that all of the important decisions in the General Assembly are really made by five principal political leaders: the governor, the president of the Senate, the Senate minority leader, the speaker of the House, and the House minority leader. In truth, these five officers frequently do meet to try to reach an agreement on a bill. They then try, usually successfully, to get enough votes from the other members of the General Assembly to pass and enact the bill into law.

The Governor and Other Top Officials

The governor and other top government leaders, such as the secretary of state, attorney general, directors of state agencies, legislative staff and the governor's aides also try to get legislation passed that they feel is important. They often try to influence legislators by the power of their position, but they can only suggest legislation; they cannot introduce bills.

On with the Game: The Citizen Player

To get on with our game, I am going to assume that you have chosen to be yourself — a citizen. On our game board (see pages 54 and 55), you will see two places to start: The path through the House and the path through the Senate. But, read the fine print: Only a representative can proceed down the House path, and only a senator can proceed down the Senate path. You cannot directly vote in this process; only the representatives and senators have that power. In Illinois, you cannot introduce a bill directly onto the board; only a representative or senator may do so.

In Illinois, the only way for citizens to bypass the General Assembly in the state lawmaking process is through citizen initiative. **Citizen initiative** is the process that citizens use to make an amendment to the state Constitution. They gather petitions signed by voters calling for a state-wide **referendum**. If enough signatures are gathered, the proposed amendment is put on the ballot in the next state election. If it passes, the propsal becomes law.

But, in Illinois, you can think of the normal lawmaking process as if it were a tag-team sporting event. For the citizen, lobbyist, governor, or party leader to get legislation passed, they must "tag" a legislator to introduce and sponsor a bill for them. To tag a legislator in this game means that you must convince the legislator that your legislation is worthwhile — that something really needs to be changed in Illinois.

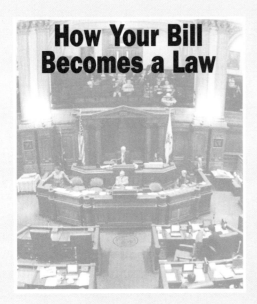

Republican James "Pate" Philip of Wood Dale (above) was the Senate president of the 91st Illinois General Assembly, while Chicago Democrat Michael J. Madigan was speaker of the House with Democrat Barbara Flynn Currie of Chicago serving as House majority leader.

Getting a Legislator to Sponsor Your Bill

Although you can suggest any legislation that you would like, let's assume that the law you would like to see passed is one that would allow fourteen-year-olds to get their driver's licenses. You must convince either your senator or your representative that this legislation is worthwhile. You only need to convince one of them to introduce your legislation, but before

How Your Bill Becomes a Law

Section 8 of Article IV of the Illinois Constitution describes how a bill becomes law. Early key steps for a bill are:
- Introduction
- First reading
- Assigned to a committee
- Committee hearings
- Committee vote

If passed by committee, a bill goes to second reading where amendments and votes on amendments are crucial. If it passes second reading, it goes to third reading where there is debate and a roll call vote. If it passes the third reading vote, it goes to the other chamber of the General Assembly, where it will follow all of the same steps. The most direct way for a bill to become law after it is passed by both the House and Senate is for the governor to sign it. ■

House of origin The chamber of the General Assembly were a bill is introduced.

Bill Proposed law presented for approval to a legislative body.

it can become a law it will have to be passed by both houses of the General Assembly. (See "How your Bill Becomes Law" on page 49.) That is why most players of the game try to get at least one sponsor for their bill in the House and at least one sponsor in the Senate.

How can you convince a representative or a senator to introduce this legislation? First, prepare your facts. Why is this legislation needed? I'm sure you can think of several reasons that you might suggest to your representative. You may write a letter, telephone, e-mail, or try to set up an appointment to meet with him or her personally. Representatives and senators have offices in their districts where you can reach them when they are not in Springfield. Let's assume that you are very convincing and that your representative chooses to introduce the legislation for you. He or she will have thought it through carefully before doing so.

Your representative would have to consider many things: how he or she feels personally about fourteen-year-olds driving, how the voters in his or her district will feel about fourteen-year-old drivers, and how different groups of people such as law enforcement groups, insurance groups, car dealers, and teachers will feel about the legislation. But remember that you are a very important person; not only are you a citizen but also you go by another title — constituent. Your representative was elected to look out for the interests of the constituents in his or her district; these constituents are the people who live in the legislator's district. The constituents who are old enough to vote (and registered to vote) can reelect him or her — or vote for someone else to represent them at the next election.

Introducing Your Bill

Let's say you succeed in tagging your representative and convincing him or her that your idea is a good one. Your representative introduces your legislation as a bill. (A bill can be introduced in either the House or the Senate. The chamber in which a bill is introduced is known as its **house of origin**.) By introducing your legislation in the House, your representative puts your bill on the game board at "Bill introduced and assigned number." What about the other side of the game board? Eventually the Senate must also deal with your legislation if it is to become a law. In the

1999 spring session of the General Assembly, lawmakers introduced 4,093 bills. Only a few hundred made it through both houses.

The first steps forward are easy to accomplish. The **bill** (or proposed law) is given a number. The number will begin with the letters "H.B." (the abbreviation for House Bill) since it is originating in the House of Representatives. The bill is placed on the calendar for future consideration. It is then read for the first time — called "1st Reading" on the game board. So far, your bill is progressing nicely, moving forward on the game board several squares.

The Rocky Road of Committee Hearings

Now comes a crucial test — one that could kill your bill. All legislation must take this rocky road known as committee hearings. Most of the study and investigation of bills takes place in committee hearings. Each bill will be assigned to a committee to be studied. The committee to which it is assigned is usually based on the content of the bill, but sometimes bills are assigned to certain committees for political reasons. Let's assume your bill was assigned to the appropriate committee, the House Committee on Transportation and Motor Vehicles.

The committee then begins the process of studying the bill. The committee must be convinced that the bill is good or your bill will die at this point and the game will be over. The committee members will hear testimony from groups who will be affected by the bill. (See "Legislative Committees' Role in Passing a Bill.")

Try to think of people who would care whether fourteen-year-olds could legally drive and you will be able to name some of the groups who might give testimony at committee hearings. Some of the people might be insurance company representatives, police officers, car dealers, school officials, and fourteen-year-olds. Lobbyists and the governor's staff will be busy at this point, too, letting the legislators know whether they support the bill.

The key legislators at the committee level are the Senate and House lead-

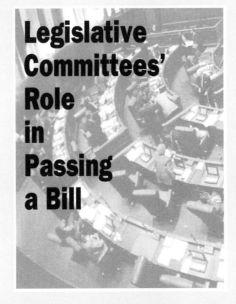

Legislative Committees' Role in Passing a Bill

Both the House and Senate have over a dozen committees made up of legislators. Almost every bill is sent first to a special committee whose job is to assign each bill to the appropriate committee for study. For example, a bill to build roads probably would go to the Transportation Committee. The chairman of the Transportation Committee would arrange for hearings on the bill with the legislator who sponsored the bill.

Hearings are study meetings to which anyone can come and present arguments for or against the bill. Finding out who among the committee members does and does not support a bill is key to preparing arguments at this stage.

After the committee studies the bill, it votes to make one of the following recommendations:

- do pass
- do pass as amended
- do not pass, or
- do not pass as amended

If the committee recommends a "do not pass," the bill is considered dead. A sponsor of a bill may appeal to all the members of his or her chamber to revive the bill, but this rarely happens. ■

ers. Think about why each of these groups might want to be represented at the committee hearings. Remember that this is one of the more dangerous sections on the game board, and it often takes cunning and political skill to get past this step.

Second Reading and the Clock is Ticking

Let's assume that your bill makes it out of committee. Your legislator now must tackle the rest of the course to get this legislation passed — and the clock is ticking. A legislative session begins in January and ends in late May or early June. That may sound like a long time, but it actually is often not enough time to get many of the bills through the game board. And if a bill doesn't make it all the way through the process in a single legislative session, then it's back to square one — provided you can find a sponsor in the next legislative session.

On the board your bill — with its legislative sponsor — has now come to a spot marked "2nd Reading." No bill may become a law unless it has made it through three readings. Can you think of reasons why those rules were included in this game?

You probably guessed that one reason was so that legislation could not hurriedly be passed through the General Assembly. Three readings give the bill a chance to be considered several times before the final vote is taken. Bills used to be actually read aloud in complete detail on three different days, but today each is read by number and a copy is printed and distributed.

Notice that one path your bill may take at second reading just drifts off into nowhere, called "Limbo land" on the game board. Some bills are just ignored — neither passed nor killed, but in limbo. There are several reasons: The legislature may run out of time; the bill's sponsor may decide that there is too much opposition to the bill; another person or lobbyist may convince the sponsor to forget the bill; or the legislative leadership might convince the sponsor not to push for further action on the bill.

Beware of the Amendment Loop

If the bill gets further consideration on second reading, there may be **amendments** proposed that could change your bill — amendments that you may or may not agree should be added. Can you think of any amendments that you would not want tacked on? What if someone added a phrase that said only straight-A students could drive at 14? Or what if, to get the needed votes to pass the bill, your legislator had to accept an amendment to the bill that said, "If a student drops out of school he or she automatically loses his or her license?"

Here is where some of those difficult decisions must be made. What if your sponsor knew that his or her constituents would not want that "dropout" amendment? Some might feel it was unconstitutional to connect driving privileges with staying in school. Others might feel that problem students would just stay in school to keep their licenses but would disrupt their classes. Other students just might want to drop out and still drive. What if your representative allows this amendment to be added? Will a lot of the people in your district be angry at your representative? Will they be angry enough to vote for someone else? What if your representative doesn't allow this amendment and the bill never gets passed? What if your representative personally likes the amendment, but knows his or her constituents don't? This is when the game gets very difficult to play, and sometimes a legislator cannot satisfy all the people he or she wants to please.

The Power of Legislative Leaders

Often, too, the governor and the legislative leadership will become very active at this second reading stage, trying to get amendments passed to the bill which will change it more to their liking. The legislative leadership may be willing to help your sponsor get this bill passed, or it may try to get your sponsor to let the bill die. The legislative leaders have very great power over what bills get passed. You might want to try to meet with some of the legislative leaders to try to convince them to support your bill. That is often a very sound part of strategy in this game.

Remember that amendments must be voted on and must receive a majority vote of the members voting before they are included as part of the bill. Sometimes so many amendments get added to a bill that the person who suggested the original bill hardly recognizes it as the same one that was introduced. That's another reason why sponsors sometimes let their bills die.

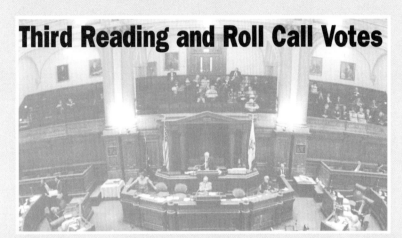

Third Reading and Roll Call Votes

Bills cannot be amended at the third reading stage, and a roll call vote is required to pass third reading. The sponsor of the bill explains the bill on the floor with all members in the chamber and briefly describes its purpose. Then, in most instances, each member is allowed five minutes to debate or question the bill. All bills require a constitutional majority to pass (30 votes in the Senate and 60 votes in the House). A roll call vote means every legislator's vote — yes, no, present, absent, or excused — is recorded by name in the official record, called House Daily Journals and Senate Daily Journals. A transcript of all floor debate and proceedings is prepared and kept for each chamber by the secretary of the Senate and by the clerk of the House. These are published and your librarian can find them for you. ∎

The Pressures at Third Reading

Let's again assume that you are lucky at second reading. Your legislator is able to keep your bill on the straight path without any really crucial amendments being added. You are now racing toward the finish line. Remember that there can be over 4,000 bills considered each session and that each step on the game board often takes a good deal of time. On the game board, you are now approaching the final hurdle (or at least it seems that way to you)—the "3rd Reading".

Up until this point your bill has been debated in committee, and it may have been debated if amendments were suggested, but now all 118 representatives have their turn to debate the bill before a final vote is taken. (See "Third Reading and Roll Call Votes.") Some bills go through third reading easily; some don't. I'm guessing your bill would cause heated debate. Some legislators would feel that it would be good

Legend:

Bill route. (This is a two-way route. Bill may begin in either House or Senate.)

Possible routes your bill may take.

Bill amended by the second house must also travel this path.

Conference committee report must pass in both houses.

Citizen   Lobbyist   Party Leader   Governor

House
of Representatives

FI

Bill becom law

Bill must have passed both the House and Senate with exact wording before going to the Governor's desk.

VETOED

Bill must return to house of origin

Bill passes

- If this bill originated in the House, then it next goes to the Senate.
- If this bill originated in the Senate and passes the House with the exact same wording, then it goes to the governor.

with amendment

Roll call vote

FAILS
Bill dies

Limbo land

Sponsor swayed by lobbyist

Sponsor changes mind

Sponsor convinced by legislator not to continue

Ran out of time

More amendments added

Influenced by state political party leaders

Amendments added

Influenced by others

2nd Reading 📖

Committee vote

Influenced by others

Amendments DANGER added

Debate

Media attention

3rd Reading 📖

Debate before all 118 representatives

Conference Committee
A conference committee of ten is created, three from the majority party and two from the minority party of each house.

FAILS
Bill dies

Committee hearings

Assigned to committee

1st Reading 📖

Bill introduced assigned number

Find legislator to sponsor bill

START HERE

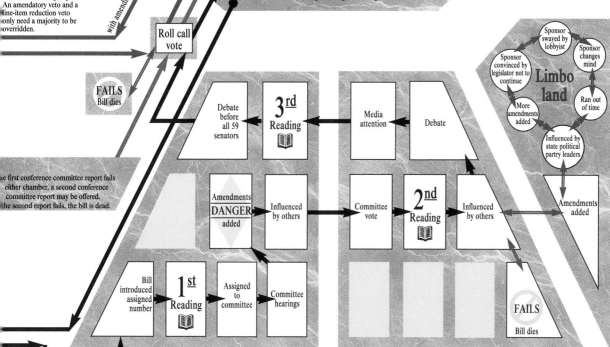

Senator Dave Syverson of Rockford discusses the nuances of a bill that he is sponsoring with Senator Bradley J. Burzynski of Sycamore.

to let fourteen-year-olds drive, and others would feel that it would be a horrible mistake. Try to argue from both sides, because to convince any opponents to change their minds you must first understand their arguments.

At this point legislators are faced with a major question for which there is no written rule. Should a legislator vote how he or she personally feels about the issue, or should he or she vote the way constituents want? What if a legislator thought that it would be great to let fourteen-year-olds drive, but that same legislator had received a lot of mail or phone calls from people in his or her district wanting a "No" vote? Which way should that legislator vote? Remember, there is no definite rule concerning what to do. Some legislators count the number of people from their district who tell them to vote "No" and the ones who tell them to vote "Yes," and then they vote the way

Conference Committees

If the Senate and the House do not pass a bill in exactly the same form, the bill has not passed. Certain things can be done, however. If one chamber has added an amendment, it is sent to the other chamber for concurrence to the amendment. If one chamber refuses to drop the amendment and the other house refuses to add it, a conference committee is formed. This committee consists of five members from the House and five from the Senate who try to write a compromise version of the bill. The compromise is called a conference committee report on the bill, and it must be approved by a constitutional majority vote in both the House and Senate in order to become law. ∎

the majority wants. Other legislators feel that they have more knowledge concerning the bill than their constituents and that they should vote what they feel is right. It is not an easy decision.

The news media will begin writing about proposed legislation as bills move through the process, especially when they come to third reading. Newspaper, television, and radio reports usually cause further reactions from citizens (including the sponsoring representatives' constituents). At the same time, the lobbyists will become very busy trying to get legislation passed or defeated, depending on how the particular group views each bill. The governor, legislative leaders, and party leaders will also use their influence again at this point to pass or defeat legislation.

Sometimes a legislator is faced with a no-win situation. He or she will be pressured to do what the lobbyists or party leaders want instead of doing what the legislator thinks his or her constituents want.

The Third Reading is Final Jeopardy

Following the debate comes the final jeopardy: All members of the House get to vote on your bill. All bills require a majority of the total membership to pass, and so you anxiously await the tally. It will take 60 "Yes" votes to pass your bill in the House. Let's say that when the count is taken, 62 representatives have voted "Yes." Your bill has passed. So you think you've won the game? No, but you have advanced to the next level. Your bill now goes automatically to the Senate, where it must go through the exact same process again.

Veto Sessions

After the General Assembly sends a bill to the governor, the governor has 60 days to decide whether to sign it, veto it, or do nothing. Because most of the bills finally passed by the General Assembly don't finish this complicated process until the last days of the session, the governor does not have time to review them — and either sign or veto them — before the General Assembly completes its work in Springfield and the members go home for the summer.

Bills that the governor signs or does nothing with become laws. Bills that the governor vetoes get one more chance. In the fall — usually in October or November — the General Assembly meets again for its fall veto session to reconsider bills the governor has vetoed totally or in part. The General Assembly can override a governor's total veto by repassing the bill with a three-fifths "super majority" in both houses. The General Assembly, however, is not limited in the fall to voting only on vetoed bills. Legislators can also introduce new legislation in a veto session.■

Game Level 2: Crossing Over to the Senate

If your bill fails anywhere along the Senate path, it will be killed even though it was so successful in the House. If your House bill gets amended in the Senate and then is passed by a majority of senators at third reading, your House bill with its Senate amendment must be repassed in the House. Remember, the rules require that both houses pass identical bills.

Sometimes when the two houses pass a similar bill, but not the exact same bill, a conference committee is formed. If successful in ironing out differences, the conference committee reports a new version of the bill, which both chambers must approve. (See "Conference Committees" on page 56.)

Vetoed Bills Must Start Over Again

Let's assume that your luck, and now skill, gets this bill through both the House and the Senate in exactly the same form. You still have not won the game. Before a bill becomes a law, it must not only pass both chambers of the General Assembly, but it must also be signed by the governor. If the governor does not like this bill, he or she may **veto** it. (Details on the governor's veto powers are in the next chapter.)

If your bill is vetoed by the governor, you still have one last chance to get your bill made into law. This usually happens in the legislature's fall veto session. (See "Veto Sessions" on page 57.) This time, however, both houses must repass your bill with a three-fifths vote. Those are the rules. In the House you would need 71 votes, and in the Senate 36 votes. Why do you suppose the Illinois Constitution was written to require more votes to repass a vetoed bill? Why would the Constitution allow the representatives and senators to pass a bill into law without the governor's approval?

I'm sure you agree with the writers of the Constitution of the State of Illinois that even with our **system of checks and balances**, it might be giving one person too much power to give him or her the final vote on every bill. However, if the chief executive were totally opposed to a bill becoming a law and yet was forced to execute it (enforce it), that would be unfair also. Therefore, the writers came up with a plan that would make it difficult to repass a bill over the governor's veto. But it is possible.

Senator Walter Dudycz takes advantage of a break in the action on the Senate floor to draft a letter to the voters back home in Chicago.

The Governor Approves Your Bill: It Becomes Law

In the actual process, it is more likely that the governor will approve your bill than veto it. So, you win! And the game is over. With the governor's signature on the bill, it becomes law. Officially it gets a Public Act number and joins all other Illinois laws, sometimes called **statutes**. You are a hero or heroine to every fourteen-year-old in the state of Illinois! No more walking to school or begging rides from older brothers or sisters. Wow! All fourteen-year-olds start dreaming of passing the state driver's test.

Wait a minute. Some reporter just called you up and said a lot of fourteen-year-olds were complaining because their older brothers and sisters did not want to share their cars, and a lot of parents were calling to complain that they just found out car insurance for fourteen-year-olds costs too much. The reporter says one parent was so upset he might file a lawsuit challenging your new law in court.

The Real Thing

Everything in this game is true, except for the bill idea we made up. It is hard to get a bill passed in the General Assembly, but the process is the best way to be certain that government works to balance what some people want against what others don't. The legislative game is just one of the games that members of the Illinois General Assembly play. Another is the constituent game.

The Constituent Game

In the constituent game, the object is to get reelected as a representative or senator. Each legislator is elected by the voters in his or her district. To get reelected to office, the legislator must earn the support of his or her constituents — the people who live in his or her district, especially those who vote.

In most districts there are people who are critical of the bills passed by the legislature and of the members who voted for them. It is not easy to get people's support and loyalty in an atmosphere where free speech and critical thinking are generally encouraged. But nobody said law-making was easy.

Winning the support of constituents is not easy, especially when there are other people in the district who would like to serve in the legislature. Candidates win office because they appeal to at least a majority of their constituents because of their political party, their cultural background, their reputation, or maybe even because of their celebrity status (like former professional wrestler Jesse Ventura who was elected governor of Minnesota in 1998). If anyone else wants to win the district and serve in the General Assembly, he or she has to defeat the person who currently holds that office — the **incumbent**. Not every incumbent runs for reelection, but they do most of the time in Illinois. How does someone beat the incumbent? The challenger will try to convince the voters in the district that the incumbent legislator is not doing a good job and that he or she can do better.

According to the Illinois Constitution, a state legislator must be a twenty-one-year-old U.S. citizen who has resided in the district from which he or she is elected for two years prior to the election. These qualifications include

Veto The word is Latin for "I forbid." A veto is the means that the governor has of preventing legislation passed by the General Assembly from becoming law.

Checks and balance system A process by which one branch of the government must oversee and approve of the action of another branch of the government. Check and balance systems make sure that no person, agency, department, or branch of government has a monopoly of power or over-reaches its mission.

Statute A law enacted by a legislature.

Incumbent A person who already holds an elected office.

Constituent work Favors or services that a legislator provides to individuals who live in his or her district.

SUM IT UP

In this chapter we have compared the work of legislators with playing two games: the legislative game and the constituent game. The legislative game is the one in which bills pass through the General Assembly: At best, to become law a bill must:

- Find a sponsor in the house of origin
- Have a first reading in the house of origin
- Go to committee in the house of origin
- Pass out of committee
- Survive the amendment danger zone
- Have a second reading in the house of origin
- Have a third reading in the house of origin
- Pass the house of origin by a majority vote
- Find a sponsor in the second house
- Have a first reading in the second house
- Go to committee in the second house
- Pass out of committee
- Survive the amendment danger zone
- Have a second reading in the second house
- Have a third reading in the second house
- Pass the second house by a majority vote
- Be signed by the governor.

The constituent game involves taking care of the people in the home district by bringing home economic goodies, such as state money to build highways and hospitals or by doing constituent work — helping people deal with the government. ■

To find out more... start with the *Governing Illinois* web site at **www.uis.edu/govern**

many people — probably because the original intent was to have part-time legislators represent the people in the General Assembly. But, in practice, many officials consider being a legislator a full-time job. In 1997, 37 percent of Illinois' 177 state legislators listed their occupations as full-time senators or representatives. Twenty-five years ago, only five percent of them thought it was a full-time job. The second biggest occupation that legislators list is attorney-at-law. In 1997, there were 41 lawyers, which was about 23 percent of all General Assembly members.

In 1997, there were nine farmers who were legislators, and around 30 legislators in some type of business, from insurance to banking to health care.

Keeping the Home District Happy

To win loyal support, legislators employ several strategies. One strategy you already know: They introduce bills that their constituents want passed. But there are other strategies as well.

Perhaps the most important of these other strategies is to get projects adopted for their districts. To win support, legislators provide all sorts of government help. They will attempt to get state government to build or improve roads in their districts, or get new parks developed, or new government buildings built. They will try to get state grants for local business and social service groups in their district.

Incumbents perform other services as well. Most legislators or their staffs spend much time on **constituent work**, which is helping people in their districts deal with state agencies. They may, for instance, help people get jobs in state government, resolve problems involving welfare assistance, get them appointments to meet with state officials, or gain admission to state hospitals or universities. They will help students find information for school assignments on state government. They would help your school make arrangements for a class trip to visit Springfield and the Capitol. Through all these services, a legislator literally becomes his or her constituents' representative in state government.

This Game's Prize: Winning Reelection

Interestingly, the more favors or services that a legislator can provide for constituents, the better his or her chances of reelection. The more often a legislator has been reelected, the more influence he or she is likely to have, and the easier it becomes to provide such services. Thus, the constituent game has a snowball effect. It is this effect which, in large part, gives incumbent legislators an advantage over their opponents in winning the next election. Winning that next election is what most state legislators want.

Local Government Legislators

Local governments also have legislators. These legislators are the elected members of the county boards, city councils, village boards, school boards, township boards, and special district boards. Like the state legislators, these local legislators make the laws for their local communities and work to provide constituent services for local residents. The work of these local legislators is described in chapter 7. ■

Chapter 5

George Ryan won the gubernatorial election in 1998 and was sworn in as the state's 39th governor on January 11, 1999.

The Governor and the Executive Branch

by Judy Lee (Lewis) Uphoff

From reading the last chapter, you know that the main function of the legislative branch is to pass new laws. Executing those laws is the main function of the executive branch. The word "executing" in the government process means carrying out or seeing that laws are put into effect. Laws would only be words on a piece of paper if the executive branch did not see that they went into effect.

Here's another way to understand executing: If you and your classmates decide to have a party, the party won't happen unless someone takes charge to see that all the arrangements are made. And you would probably want that someone to make sure the party doesn't cost more than you plan to spend.

TERRIFYING! HORRIFIC!!

ITS FILLED WITH THE CANDIDATES FOR STATE OFFICES!!!

VOTERS

HAUNTED HOUSE

THOMPSON

Electing Illinois' Six Executives

For our national government there are only two elected executive officials, the president and the vice president. But, in Illinois, voters elect six state government executive officials: the governor, the lieutenant governor, the secretary of state, the attorney general, the treasurer, and the comptroller. Each is elected in even-numbered years that are not presidential election years. They serve four-year terms. To be eligible for each of the executive offices of Illinois, candidates must be U.S. citizens, at least 25 years old, and residents of the state for the three years before the election.

Election of the six **executive branch** officials is a two-step process, and in Illinois the elections are very political. First, there are **primary elections** held in March of an election year by the Republican and Democratic parties. The purpose of the primary elections is for each party to nominate its candidates for each office. Then there is the **general election** in November when all voters choose between the Republican, Democratic, and any third-party candidates. Each of these executive officials is elected independently of the others, except that the governor and the lieutenant governor candidates of each party must run as a team in the general election. There is no such team requirement in the primaries. (For more information, see "Primary and General Elections" on the next page.)

A team requirement prevents election of the governor from one party and the lieutenant governor from another. Because no other candidate for executive office is teamed to the governor, it is not only possible, but probable, that the state's other elected executive officers will be from different parties. For example, in 1998, the Republican candidates won election to the offices of governor, lieutenant governor, attorney general, and treasurer, while the Democratic candidates won election to the offices of secretary of state and comptroller.

The Office of Governor

Of all the officials in the Illinois executive branch, the governor is the most prestigious and most powerful. The governor is the chief executive officer of the state of Illinois. Shadrach Bond was the first governor, chosen in 1818 when Illinois became a state. Because citizens in our state

Executive branch One of the three branches of Illinois government. This branch is charged with carrying out laws enacted by the legislative branch of government. There are six elected executive branch officers in Illinois: the governor, lieutenant governor, attorney general, secretary of state, comptroller, and treasurer.

Primary election An election in which members of the same party run in order to win their party's nomination for an elected office. Only party members may vote in a primary election.

General election An election in which the winners of the party primaries and perhaps independent candidates run for a public office. All eligible, registered voters may vote in a general election no matter what party they belong to.

still feared rule by kings, early state constitutions would not allow the governor to run for two terms in a row. So, by 1999 Illinois has had 39 governors. The current state Constitution allows governors to run for as many terms as they wish. The governor who has been elected the most times is James R. Thompson, who first took office in January 1977 after the 1976 election. He was elected four times.

But let's get back to the idea of executing the law. Once a bill becomes law, the governor must see that it is carried out. That is the governor's primary job. Of course, it would be impossible for one person to carry out all the laws of the state. The governor has about 63,000 employees to help, working throughout various executive agencies, departments, commissions, and authorities. The other elected executive officials and their employees also help carry out some of the laws. Each one of these different executive offices has a special job to do and certain laws to enforce.

The Governor's Role in Lawmaking

Besides carrying out the laws, the governor also plays a big role in making the laws and affecting public policy. The governor is not a member of the General Assembly, so the governor cannot directly introduce or vote on legislation. But the governor's executive powers and standing as a political leader give the governor much influence over which bills become laws.

Every year in January the governor makes a speech to the General Assembly called the

Primary and General Elections

In general, each successful candidate for a state government office in Illinois—in both the legislative and executive branches—must win two elections. First, a candidate must win his or her party's nomination for the office. This is accomplished by winning a primary election.

In the March primary, each party picks its candidates for office. Usually the Democratic Party and the Republican Party are the major political parties holding primaries. Other parties—generically called "third parties"— can also nominate candidates to run in the general election.

Let's consider a typical Illinois primary. Let's say there are three Democrats who want to run for governor. They will run against each other in the Democratic primary election. On the same day at the same polling places throughout the state, Republicans who want to be governor will run against each other in the Republican Party primary election. In Illinois, voters must declare at the polling place which primary ballot they want—Republican, Democrat, or any third party that has candidates. The Democrat who wins the most votes for governor in the Democratic primary wins the party nomination for governor and begins the campaign for the November general election against the Republican who won the Republican Party nomination in the Republican primary and any third-party candidate who won his or her party's nomination.

Sometimes there is no competition at the party primaries for one or more of the state offices. But there always is competition in the November election, called the general election.

In the general election, voters do not need to declare which party they support. All voters are given ballots that have the names of the Democratic, Republican, and third-party nominees for each office. Relatively few voters vote only for the nominees of just one party. Most often, voters split their vote: voting for the Republican for governor but the Democrat for secretary of state, for example.

Historically, third-party candidates have little chance of winning statewide elections, but if the election is close for one of the offices between the candidate of Republican and Democratic parties, then a third-party candidate could draw just enough votes to have a major influence on which candidate wins the election and becomes our new state official.

In all Illinois elections, the candidate who gets the most votes is the winner. ■

"State of the State" speech The address that the governor gives at the opening of each session of the General Assembly. In this speech the governor outlines the new laws he or she wants the legislature to pass that year.

Veto The word is Latin for "I forbid." A veto is the means that the governor has of preventing legislation passed by the General Assembly from becoming law. The governor of Illinois has four types of vetoes: total, line-item, reduction, and amendatory.

Appropriation bills Legislative bills that permit spending of the state's money.

Line-item veto A type of veto whereby the governor can say no to one or more lines listing spending amounts for specific programs or projects in an appropriations bill while still signing the remainder of the bill into law.

Reduction veto A type of veto whereby the governor can reduce the amount of money spent for specific programs or projects in an appropriations bill.

Amendatory veto A type of veto whereby the governor can write changes into bills that the General Assembly has passed.

Override The process that the General Assembly has in order to make a bill become a law after the governor has vetoed it. Overriding the governor's veto requires a three-fifths majority in both the Senate and the House of Representatives.

State budget The state's financial plan, it details the money that the state is expected to receive and the way the state expects to spend the money.

Balanced budget A budget in which the state plans to spend no more than it takes in.

"State of the State." In this speech the governor suggests to the legislators what legislation to pass. The governor also persuades legislators to introduce bills. The governor has staff assistants who lobby the members of the General Assembly, trying to convince them to approve the bills favored by the governor. When a bill is approved by the General Assembly, it goes to the governor who may sign it into law or veto it.

The Governor's Powers to Veto

By using the governor's power to veto bills passed by the General Assembly — or threatening to use it — the governor can often pressure the General Assembly to approve legislation in the form that the governor prefers.

The governor of Illinois has more kinds of veto powers than the president of the United States does. Both have the power to **veto** an entire bill, sending it back to the legislature. But the Illinois governor has three other kinds of vetoes. The Illinois governor has two ways to veto bills that authorize spending (called **appropriation bills**) and another veto power that allows the governor to write changes into bills.

The first veto power related to appropriations bills is the **line-item veto**, which is the power the governor has to veto one or more lines of spending amounts for specific programs or projects in one bill, yet the governor can sign the rest of the bill into law. The lines crossed out by the governor are considered vetoed, and that money cannot be spent unless the General Assembly repasses the bill with a three-fifths vote in both the Senate and the House.

The second veto power related to appropriations bills is called the **reduction veto**. With this power, the governor may reduce the amount of money to be spent for a specific program or project. Such a reduction cannot be restored to the amount approved by the General Assembly unless both the House and the Senate reapprove the original amount by a majority vote.

The other veto power allows the governor to write changes into the bills that passed the General Assembly. This power is called the **amendatory veto**. It allows the governor to write proposed amendments, but only to bills already approved by the General Assembly. This power adds a new dimension to the legislative game described in chapter 4. To go back to the example in that chapter, what if the governor decided not to sign your bill allowing fourteen-year-olds to get driver's licenses? Let's say the governor decided to use the amendatory veto, returning your bill to the General Assembly with a suggested amendment to allow only fourteen-year-olds who are not failing any schoolwork to get a driver's license.

Three things could happen when a bill is returned to the General Assembly with an amendatory veto:

1. The General Assembly could **override** the veto. To do this, the General Assembly must repass the original bill. But, a three-fifths vote of both houses is required for the original bill to become law. If the General Assembly does repass the bill under those conditions, the veto is overridden and the bill becomes law.
2. The General Assembly could approve the governor's changes to the

bill. A majority vote, not the three-fifths, is needed in both houses for the bill as the governor amended it to become law.

3. The General Assembly could fail to vote either way, and the bill dies.

On the other hand, if the governor neither signs nor in any way amends or vetoes a bill, that bill will become law automatically sixty days after it was sent to the governor. The opposite is true if the president of the United States neither signs nor vetoes a bill passed by Congress: The bill is considered vetoed.

Some people believe that the veto powers, particularly the amendatory veto, give the Illinois governor too much power and influence over lawmaking. Others believe that these veto powers are necessary because the General Assembly passes so many bills in the last days of the annual spring session that it does make mistakes, and the governor can correct any mistakes with vetoes. More important to some is that these veto powers allow the governor to be a strong executive leader, providing a focus for state government decision-making.

The Governor's Budget Powers

The governor also has important powers over the way the state spends its money. With these powers, the governor can influence and control the kinds of services that the residents of Illinois receive from the state. Only the General Assembly can authorize spending by its approval of appropriations bills, but the governor's line-item and reduction veto powers can make it harder for the General Assembly to reapprove the spending.

Each year, it is the governor who kicks off the process of deciding how much the state will spend on each and every program of the state government. In March each year, the governor presents a budget speech that outlines a plan for the state's public policy activities along with a plan for financing them. The plan is called the **state budget**, and the governor must balance spending against revenue or income. A **balanced budget** means the state will spend no more money in that year than the state expects to receive that year in revenues from taxes, license fees, and other revenue sources.

To prepare the budget, the governor must first figure out how much money the state of Illinois will receive. That's the total revenue. Then the governor divides up that amount for spending by all the state offices and agencies. Because the state is responsible for providing so many services to its citizens, the list for spending is extremely long. There is education in schools like yours, and in all the state colleges and universities. There are roads and bridges to build or repair. There are some people who need welfare programs for food, housing, clothes, and hospital bills. There are prisons and mental health workers. Workers want good benefits if they are hurt on the job or help if they lose their jobs. Children need help if someone abuses them. State police are needed to patrol highways. Local governments want financial help from the state, too.

The governor's budget provides money for projects that people need, from schools to police protection to road construction.

Each agency in Illinois that is funded by the state of Illinois must convince the governor to budget the money it thinks it needs to provide its services. Unless the governor asks for more taxes to increase the revenue side of the budget, there usually is not enough money to spend to satisfy everyone.

The governor sends his budget to the General Assembly, and the General Assembly must authorize all spending by passing appropriation bills. If taxes are proposed, only the General Assembly can approve them. The members of the General Assembly often disagree with the governor's plan for state spending; they also sometimes disagree with the governor's revenue predictions. Finally, the General Assembly passes appropriation bills authorizing spending for the year. If the governor does not like the spending authorized by the General Assembly, the governor can veto appropriation bills (but he or she cannot increase them).

The governor still has one other important power over spending: the **allocation of funds**. This means that the governor can still cut back state spending authorized by the General Assembly if the state's income is less than predicted. In short, the governor can order agencies not to spend the money appropriated to them in the budget.

The Governor's Other Powers

The governor holds much power over state government. In addition to setting the policy direction of the state, proposing its budget, and using veto power, the governor can also:

• make appointments
• issue pardons
• issue executive orders
• call out the National Guard, and
• call special sessions of the General Assembly.

The governor appoints the people who run the executive administrative agencies, boards, commissions, and authorities—subject to approval by the Senate. We will talk further about these agencies and boards later in the chapter, but basically the agencies, boards, and departments are the structures that help the governor execute the laws. If the governor wants to rearrange the powers of the executive agencies, the governor has the power to reorganize them—subject only to the disapproval of either the Senate or the House.

The way the governor rearranges the departments or agencies is usually accomplished by issuing an **executive order**. An executive order looks very much like a legislative bill, only it does not have to pass through the General Assembly unless it conflicts with an existing law. Generally, you can think of executive orders as the way the governor tells employees how to get their jobs done, or how they must behave as the governor's employees. For example, in 1999, Governor George Ryan ordered that people who worked for the governor would not be allowed to contribute money to his campaign fund.

The governor may also grant **pardons** to people who have been convicted of crimes in Illinois. And the governor serves as commander-in-chief of the state militia (the Illinois National Guard), which can be called out by the governor's order to help if there is a disaster or emergency (or by the president if there is a national emergency and it is needed to help the U.S. Army). Also, if the General Assembly is in recess, the governor can call the legislature, or just the Senate, into a **special session** to deal with legislation on specific topics. For example, if there were to be a budget shortfall, the governor could call the General Assembly together to consider bills on reducing state spending or increasing taxes, but no other legislation could be brought forward in that special session.

Allocation of funds The process by which the state allows money to be spent by agencies.

Executive order A power the governor uses to make rules for the agencies and people who work for the governor.

Pardon A power that allows the governor either (1) to excuse someone accused or convicted of a crime from legal responsibility for the criminal action, or (2) to reduce or eliminate the punishment the courts have imposed on someone convicted of a crime.

Special session An extraordinary meeting of the General Assembly that the governor calls so that the legislature may consider action on certain, specific topics.

Other Executive Officers

Each of the other five elected executive officials have special duties. We will study these five in the order that their offices would appear on a general election ballot.

The Lieutenant Governor

Corinne Wood, elected in 1998, is the state's first female lieutenant governor.

The lieutenant governor is assigned duties by the governor. Some governors expect the lieutenant governor to do lots of work and others expect very little. The lieutenant governor's job can best be described as an assistant to the governor. The lieutenant governor takes over for the governor when the governor is unable to fulfill the duties, just as the vice president takes over for the president of the United States. Unlike the vice president, who presides over the U.S. Senate and has the power to vote in the Senate to break a tie vote, Illinois' lieutenant governor has no such role.

The Attorney General

The attorney general is the chief legal officer for the state of Illinois. If Illinois is sued, the attorney general is the state's lawyer. If Illinois as a state must sue because someone did not fulfill a state contract or agreement, the attorney general is the state's lawyer. The attorney general also issues legal opinions for government officials who question new laws or conflicts between state laws. The attorney general keeps records of consumer fraud and helps citizens if they think they have been cheated by a business.

Attorney General Jim Ryan is the state's chief legal officer.

The Secretary of State

The secretary of state keeps official records for the state of Illinois. Those records include all the proceedings and decisions of the General Assembly, and all the records on motor vehicle licenses and driver's licenses in Illinois. The offices where you go to take your driver's license test or to get a new driver's license are run by the secretary of state.

The secretary of state is the state archivist and the state librarian. The official state library is administered by the secretary of state, and its literacy programs are available throughout Illinois.

The secretary of state also keeps the records of all rules and regulations that are made by executive branch agencies in carrying out the laws. These are called administrative rules.

The secretary of state's office has become one of the largest and most influential of all of the executive offices. As the population of Illinois has grown and with its duty of keeping the official records of the state, the office has expanded in duties and in prestige. This office probably is the office that most people in the state have the most direct contact with. As a result, the office has recently become a stepping stone to greater things. For example both Governor Edgar and Governor Ryan served as secretary of state immediately before winning election to the governor's office. The duties of the secretary of state's office, while expanding, must comply with the framework intended by the authors of the Constitution.

Jesse White was elected secretary of state in 1998. The duties of the office include issuing license plates and acting as the state's archivist and librarian.

The State Comptroller

The office of comptroller is one of the newest and may be one of the shortest in existence. The office was established by the Constitution of 1970. It took the place of an old position called the auditor of public accounts. The intent was to create an additional **check and balance system** on our public treasury. Following some scandals involving state finances, the writers of the 1970 Constitution felt that all public spending required approval from the office of the comptroller before a check could be issued from the office of the treasurer. While this system, in theory, provides a good way to deter misspending, the extra layer of bureaucracy caused by having two state financial officers (the treasurer and comptroller) can slow down the bill paying process. In 1998, both houses of the General Assembly passed bills that would have combined the offices of comptroller and treasurer into one

Check and balance system A process by which one department or branch of the government must oversee and approve of the action of another department or branch of the government. Check and balance systems make sure that no person, agency, department, or branch of government has a monopoly of power or overreaches its mission.

Dan Hynes is the state comptroller. The comptroller's office manages the state's financial accounts by recording transactions, processing data, performing audits, issuing financial reports, and providing leadership on the fiscal affairs of the state.

office. But, the General Assembly couldn't agree on a single bill, so the merger didn't happen. But ideas to reform Illinois government hardly ever die, so the office of the comptroller may one day be history.

The State Treasurer

In Illinois the executive official who actually writes the checks that pay the state's bills is the treasurer. The treasurer also is responsible for the safekeeping and investment of state money.

How the State's Executives Work Together

Consider how your bill that was passed into law in chapter 4 would involve the executive branch officials. What would it take to carry out the law for fourteen-year-olds to get licenses to drive? The governor would have to provide funds in the budget to hire new driver's license examiners to test fourteen-year-olds. The secretary of state would have to hire people to fill these jobs, train them, and assign them to driver's license examining stations. The comptroller would check to be sure

Judy Baar Topinka was first elected state treasurer in 1994. As the state's banker, she is responsible for the safekeeping of taxpayers' money and investing it wisely.

that these persons were officially on the job and review the vouchers from the secretary of state's office for paying their salaries. The comptroller would then tell the treasurer to issue a state check to pay them their salaries. The treasurer would write the checks (or would oversee the electronic writing of these checks) for these examiners. Meanwhile, the attorney general might be defending the new law in court because a fourteen-year-old Illinois driver sideswiped a fire truck in Missouri, where you have to be 16 to drive a car.

Even though the state executive officials might be from different political parties, once they are elected they must work together to perform their different duties to see that all state laws are faithfully enforced.

The Auditor General

Two of the state's financial officers are the treasurer and the comptroller. They are popularly elected officials in the executive branch of the state government. The state's third financial officer is the auditor general. The auditor general is an officer of the legislative branch and is appointed by the General Assembly for a ten-year term of office. The auditor general is *not* an executive branch officer.

The auditor general's job is to review the spending of all state funds to see that all money is spent in accordance with the law. The auditor general also reviews the performance of the executive branch—or how agencies carry out the laws of the state—to be sure that neither more nor less is done than the laws provide. The auditor general is like a watchdog for the General Assembly, checking especially that the executive branch is doing its job and spending state funds according to the laws and the Constitution. ■

The Administrative Departments

So far we have discussed only the top state elected officials. All of the six elected executive officials have offices in Springfield and Chicago. The governor, as noted at the beginning of this chapter, has by far the most help. These are the 63,000 state employees who work in over 70 executive departments, agencies, boards, commissions, and authorities under the governor's control. Some of these offices are large and some are small. For example, the Department of Corrections, which administers state prisons, has about 15,500 employees; the Illinois Racing Board, which regulates horse racing in Illinois, has approximately 140 employees.

The Code Departments

Most of the state's services and programs are provided by the state's code departments. They are called code departments because each is created and its powers and duties are established by one set of state laws, called the **administrative code**. This code also includes some laws applying to all the departments. For example, it sets up the personnel code or **civil service system** under which most of the employees of these departments and others under the governor are supposed to be hired, retained, promoted, and dismissed.

The **code departments** are the agencies through which the state provides most of its services to its citizens. The code departments include, for example, the Department of Transportation, which builds and maintains state highways; the Department of Public Aid, which administers welfare programs; the Department of Corrections, which manages the state's prison system; and the Department of Agriculture, which provides assistance to farmers and operates the State Fairs in Springfield and DuQuoin. Code departments are listed on the next page. Your teacher may have a copy of the *Handbook of Illinois,* which describes the major state agencies. Every detail about executive government is spelled out in the statutes of Illinois government.

Each of these department directors is appointed by the governor, and confirmed by the Senate. The directors are similar to the president's cabinet of the U.S. government.

Executive Boards

Not all the other Illinois executive or administrative departments are set up with one top person who has the power to make the major decisions. Illinois has many boards and commissions, whose members are appointed by the governor, often with

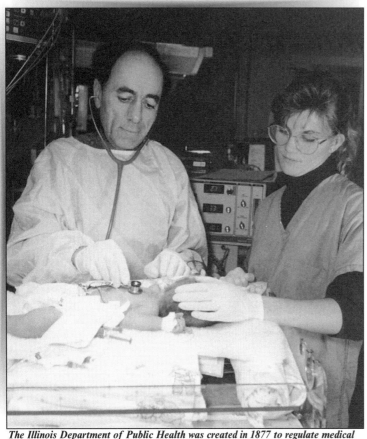

The Illinois Department of Public Health was created in 1877 to regulate medical practitioners and to promote sanitation. Today, it is responsible for protecting the state's 11.9 million residents through the prevention and control of disease and injury. The range of public health services runs from vaccinations to protect children against disease; to testing to assure the safety of food, water, and drugs; to licensing health care facilities and professionals to ensure quality care in hospitals and nursing homes.

A seed lab employee examines seed samples for the Department of Agriculture. She is checking for noxious weed tolerance levels.

the consent of the Senate. The members of the board make the major decisions, and usually the board appoints a person as the director in charge of all the employees who work for the board.

Some of these boards are for education. One of the most important is the State Board of Education, which coordinates all public education from preschool through grade twelve. The board appoints the state superintendent of education, who administers all the programs and the employees of the State Board of Education.

There is a separate Illinois Board of Higher Education, which coordinates the state's higher education system. That system includes the Illinois Student Assistance Commission, which grants financial aid; the Illinois Community College Board, which assists all the local community colleges in the state; and nine different university governing boards that run the state's nine universities. Each of the university boards seeks approval for its budget and new programs through the Illinois Board of Higher Education.

The Governor's Bureau of the Budget

An important state agency is the Bureau of the Budget. This agency is part of the governor's office staff. It works directly for the governor, who gets to hire the director and staff. This bureau helps the governor prepare the state budget. Every other agency sends its budget requests to the Bureau of the Budget. This agency helps the governor both to regulate state spending and to check if revenues will be enough for the state to do all its business throughout the year. The director of the Bureau of the Budget is one of the most important advisers working directly for the governor.

Illinois' Code Departments

Department on Aging

Department of Agriculture

Department of Central Management Services

Department of Children and Family Services

Department of Commerce and Community Affairs

Department of Corrections

Department of Employment Security

Department of Financial Institutions

Department of Human Rights

Department of Human Services

Department of Insurance

Department of Labor

Department of Lottery

Department of Natural Resources

Department of Nuclear Safety

Department of Professional Regulation

Department of Public Aid

Department of Public Health

Department of Revenue

Department of State Police

Department of Transportation

Department of Veterans' Affairs

For more information on the code departments and other state agencies, check the State of Illinois web site at www.state.il.us.

SUM IT UP

The state's executive branch is made up of the state's elected executive branch officers and the agencies and departments that the governor oversees. The state's executive officers are the:

- governor
- lieutenant governor
- attorney general
- secretary of state
- comptroller, and
- treasurer.

No executive officer or agency can make laws, but the governor has the power to shape laws by means of a veto. The governor has four veto powers:

1. total veto
2. line-item veto
3. reduction veto, and
4. amendatory veto.

The job of the executive branch and its officers is to make sure that laws are put into practice. The job is accomplished not only by the six executive officers, but also by the offices, departments, agencies, boards, and commissions that are overseen by executive branch officers. ■

To find out more...
start with the *Governing Illinois* web site at **www.uis.edu/govern**

The National Guard can be called out by the governor to help in case of floods or other emergencies. It can also be called out by the president to join the nation's regular armed forces.

Other Agencies, Boards, and Commissions

The importance of all the departments, agencies, boards, commissions, and authorities to any one citizen may depend on his or her interests. In carrying out the laws, these departments and agencies also may make administrative rules. The rules help provide detailed guidelines for the laws passed by the legislature.

Another important board appointed by the governor is the State Board of Elections, which administers all of the election laws of the state. It keeps the official results of all the state elections.

The Illinois National Guard is run by the Department of Military Affairs, which is headed by the state's adjutant general. The National Guard, as the state's militia, can be called out by the governor to help in case of severe floods or other emergencies. It can also be subject to order by the president, as commander-in-chief of the U.S. military, to be called out to join the nation's regular armed forces.

The state has two important agencies in the environmental field. One is the Illinois Environmental Protection Agency and the other is the Pollution Control Board.

There are boards that regulate certain activities for the state: horse racing, liquor sales, and utility rates on electricity, and telephone calls, to name a few. There is a commissioner who regulates state banks and real estate professionals.

There are agencies involved in public safety such as the state fire marshal and the Emergency Management Agency.

Interested in the arts or historic preservation? There is an Illinois Arts Council and a Historic Preservation Agency.

The operation of such a vast administrative organization in the Illinois executive branch is a big enterprise. Indeed, the state spends billions each year operating state government and providing services to Illinois residents through these many agencies. Many state services are provided indirectly through local governments. Most programs, from the Department of Public Aid for example, are provided to the people from county offices. ■

Chapter 6

This statue depicting the seat of justice flanks the steps of the Illinois State Supreme Court building in Springfield.

The Courts and the Concept of Law

by Denny L. Schillings

Law is an important and common part of our everyday lives, but we seldom give much thought to it. In general terms, the law is a set of rules that allows human beings to live together in some kind of orderly manner. Laws have been around as long as mankind. Some of the earliest references to written laws come from ancient history. King Hammurabi, of ancient Babylon, formally established a code of law

Law A rule of conduct or procedure established by custom, agreement, or authority.

Common law The system of laws originated and developed in England and based on court decisions, customs, and usage rather than on written laws.

Federalism A system of government in which power is divided between a central authority and constituent political units, known as states in the U. S. system.

Civil law Laws dealing with the rights of private citizens.

Contract An agreement between two or more parties that is usually written and enforceable by law.

Criminal law Laws that govern acts by which a person may be punished by imprisonment.

Misdemeanor A criminal offense less serious than a felony and usually punishable by a fine, probation, or a short jail term.

Felony Serious crimes, such as murder, rape, or burglary, punishable by a more stringent sentence than that given for a misdemeanor.

before his death in 1750 B.C. The Greeks philosophized about the effect of good and bad laws. Roman law was a keystone in the rule of the empire. Written, organized, and generally accepted laws written by legislatures, like the ones we are accustomed to, are relatively new to world history, however.

While using many of the ideas of the Greeks, Romans, and others, the framers of our U.S. Constitution looked most often to England. By the year 1150 A.D., the English were living under a government with a single ruler, and laws were applied throughout the nation. A variety of

The courts both interpret the laws and decide the guilt or innocence of people charged with breaking them. Without the courts, laws are just a stack of dusty books on a shelf.

laws, called the **common law**, had been developing for centuries and were established for all to follow as judges made decisions in England.

You have learned that our laws are passed by the representatives of the people — the Congress and the state legislatures or county boards and municipal councils. But it is the courts that both interpret the laws and decide the guilt and innocence of people charged with breaking the laws.

The basic concept of **federalism** that we studied in chapter 3 is easily identified in our court system. Our national court system deals with federal law and interprets the U.S. Constitution. The state courts interpret state and local laws and the state Constitution. Some cases from state courts can also be appealed through the federal system. Any time a state or local law is challenged as being in violation of the U.S. Constitution, the case may go through the federal judiciary. But, for the most part, the state and local laws that govern our everyday lives are left up to the state courts.

Civil and Criminal Law

Laws are divided into two broad types. State courts deal with both. The first, **civil law**, involves disputes between two or more individuals or groups. If you were involved in an automobile accident and sued the other person for

Both civil and criminal law cases are heard in the state's courtrooms such as those found in the Macoupin County Courthouse in Carlinville.

damages, it would be a civil law case. Another example could involve a **contract**. Assume your mother signed a contract to have a new roof put on your house, and the roofer did not complete the work. Your mother might bring a civil suit against the roofer to get her money back or force the roofer to finish the job. In both examples the civil law involved deals with relationships between individuals, not crimes.

Criminal law is the other type. When citizens actually break a law, the state brings charges against them. A **misdemeanor** is a crime that is not too serious, and it does not involve a large fine or long jail term. Shoplifting is an example. If found guilty, the person might be sentenced to probation or fined. The punishment is meant to discourage the person from criminal actions in the future.

A **felony**, on the other hand, is a serious criminal act, such as robbery, murder, or arson. Felonies have much more severe penalties than misdemeanors. Long prison terms and large fines are common for those convicted of a felony. A person who has committed a felony is said to have harmed society as a whole, and the punishment is meant to protect society from further injury.

The Judicial System in Illinois

Article VI of the Illinois Constitution establishes a system of courts for the state. In many ways the state court system is similar in purpose and structure to that of the federal system. The federal and state judiciaries are known as the third branches of government — giving both the U.S. and Illinois an executive branch, a legislative branch, and a judicial branch. This third branch was created to adhere to the separation of powers doctrine, which is a concept that allows for checks and balances to the powers of the executive and legislative branches of the government. Both state and federal judicial systems have three basic levels; both interpret the constitution for their respective jurisdictions; and both are responsible for deciding individual cases that come before them.

There are also differences between the state and federal court systems. The responsibilities of the federal court system are broadly defined because its decisions affect all the states, as well as other countries, as it interprets and applies federal laws and the U.S. Constitution. The responsibility of the Illinois court system, on the other hand, is rather detailed because it deals with state laws that concern nearly all aspects of our lives. Another differ-

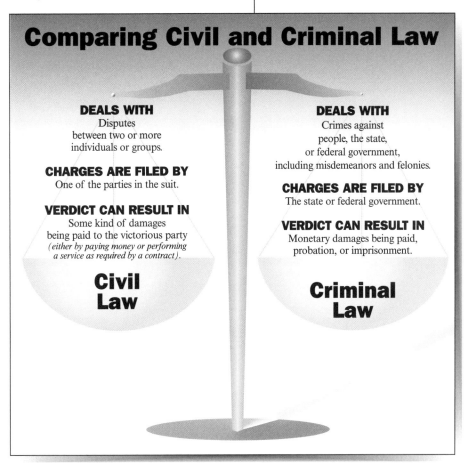

Comparing Civil and Criminal Law

DEALS WITH
Disputes
between two or more
individuals or groups.

CHARGES ARE FILED BY
One of the parties in the suit.

VERDICT CAN RESULT IN
Some kind of damages
being paid to the victorious party
*(either by paying money or performing
a service as required by a contract).*

Civil Law

DEALS WITH
Crimes against
people, the state,
or federal government,
including misdemeanors and felonies.

CHARGES ARE FILED BY
The state or federal government.

VERDICT CAN RESULT IN
Monetary damages being paid,
probation, or imprisonment.

Criminal Law

ence between the state and federal judiciary is the number and type of courts. The U.S. Congress is given power to create lower courts if it thinks they are needed. In Illinois, the entire court system is set out in the state Constitution; the General Assembly cannot create any other courts. A final difference is that judges in Illinois are elected for a specific term of office, whereas federal judges are appointed for life. Illinois' system of elected judges is discussed later in this chapter.

The federal judicial system was set up in Article III of the U.S. Constitution. A nine-member Supreme Court is empowered to make final judgment on cases appealed to it. Any other federal courts were left up to Congress to establish, and it did so in 1789 by passing the Judiciary Act.

The act created a system of lower federal courts to assist the Supreme Court in dealing with federal laws. In each state there is at least one U.S. district court, and most federal cases start at this level. For Illinois there are three U.S. district courts. The Northern District has divisions in Chicago and Rockford; the Central District has divisions in Peoria, Springfield, Rock Island, Urbana, and Danville; and the Southern District has offices in East St. Louis, and Benton. If the decision of a district court is challenged, the case goes up to the next level—to one of thirteen U.S. courts of appeals. A challenge to a decision of the appeals court would be reviewed by the Supreme Court. But, the Supreme Court can refuse to hear any particular case, leaving the appeals court ruling as the final decision. In addition, Congress has created a number of specialized courts, such as military courts, the U.S. Court of International Trade, and the U.S. Tax Court. It is the U.S. Supreme Court that makes the final decisions on any challenges made to decisions of these courts.

In the Illinois judiciary system there are three levels of courts:

Comparing the Federal Judicial System and the Illinois Judicial System

Federal judicial system	Illinois judicial system
Created by Article III of the Constitution of the United States.	**Created by** Article VI of the 1970 Constitution of the State of Illinois.
The court system Is composed of three levels as established by the Constitution and, for the lower courts, the Congress. The three levels are: • The Supreme Court • Court of appeals • District courts	**The court system** Is composed of three basic levels as set forth in Article VI of the 1970 Constitution of the State of Illinois. The three levels are: • The state Supreme Court • The state appellate courts • The circuit courts
Judges are Selected for life.	**Judges are** Elected for a specific term of office.
The Supreme Court The U.S. Supreme Court interprets the Constitution of the United States by hearing certain cases that are appealed to it after they have been ruled on by a U.S. court of appeals (though sometimes cases can come from state appellate courts). The Supreme Court is made up of nine justices selected for life by the president of the United States with the advice and consent of the U. S. Senate.	**The Supreme Court** The Illinois Supreme Court interprets the 1970 Constitution of the State of Illinois by hearing cases that are appealed to it after they have been ruled on by a state appellate court. However, for cases on some specific topics (see Article VI, Section 4(a)), the Supreme Court exercises original jurisdiction. Also, the Supreme Court must hear appeals from circuit court cases for which the death penalty has been handed down. The Illinois Supreme Court is made up of seven justices who are elected for ten-year terms of office in general or judicial elections.

- Circuit courts
- Appellate courts
- The Illinois Supreme Court.

Let's take a detailed look at each level of the state's judicial system.

Circuit Courts

The lowest level of Illinois' three-tiered court system is the circuit court, sometimes called trial courts. Circuit courts hear cases of all kinds, from divorces to murders. The circuit courts have **original jurisdiction** in both civil and criminal cases. That means the circuit courts are the first courts where both civil and criminal cases are tried. They are the most numerous of all the state courts. The state is divided into 22 areas called judicial circuits, and each contains one or more counties. Cook County, by far the most heavily populated county in the state, has its own circuit. DuPage County, the second most populous county, also has its own circuit, as does Will County. The other nineteen circuits contain two or more counties.

The Constitution states that there will be at least one circuit court judge for every county. For Cook County, at least 36 circuit judges must come from Chicago, and at least 12 must come from the rest of the county. It is left up to the General Assembly to provide for more circuit court judges, and it has. In 1997, there were 49 resident circuit court judges and 97 at large circuit court judges in Cook County. There were 227 circuit court judges holding court in the other 21 circuits. Circuit court judges are elected by the voters in their circuit for six-year terms. They are nominated in their political party's primary election, and, to become judge, must win the general election. If they want to serve another term, their names go directly on the general election ballot and no one can run against them. Instead, voters mark the ballot either yes or no to retain the judge for another term. Three-fifths or more of the voters actually voting on the question of the judge's retention must vote in favor of retaining the judge for the judge to get another term.

The Illinois Constitution also provides for another type of circuit court judge, called associate judges. They are appointed by the elected circuit court judges for a term of four years. Some people criticize how the appointments are made, since there are no guarantees the person appointed will make a good judge. Of course, since circuit court judges are elected through the political process, this leads to other criticism that these judges could be too political.

The associate judge's role in the circuit court system is to hear cases concerning traffic tickets, charges of disorderly conduct, drunk driving, and other offenses that carry less severe penalties than other more serious offenses. In 1997 there were 221 associate circuit judges in the circuits outside of Cook County. Because of their role in dealing with minor offenses, associate judges are the most familiar to many Illinois residents.

In order for the circuit court system to serve the public better, each circuit is divided into divisions. One division may hear felony cases, another only juvenile cases, and another only divorces. As cases come to the circuit court, the chief judge of the circuit assigns each to a specific court

Original jurisdiction The court in which civil and criminal cases are first heard.

The Illinois Court System in Action

This chapter looks at the various parts of the judicial system in Illinois, but an example of how it works in a criminal case should help you understand it better.

Bill Small was a nineteen-year-old high school dropout. After three years of part-time jobs he was unemployed and broke. In order to get money, he decided to rob a neighborhood gas station. On a Monday night, just after eleven, Bill put on a Halloween mask, and set out to gain quick money.

As he walked toward the gas station, Bill was not aware that a city police officer on routine patrol had spotted him. Bill forced the attendant on duty to empty the cash register. Then Bill ran out of the station with the money in his pocket. The police were waiting outside.

"Drop your weapon," the police officer commanded.

"I don't have one," answered Bill.

The officer arrested him, reading to Bill his rights at the same time: He could remain silent; any answers he gave could be used against him in court; he could be represented by an attorney; and, if he could not afford an attorney, one would be provided free.

The officer then asked, "Do you understand these rights?"

Bill said, "Yes."

Handcuffed and riding in the back of the squad car, Bill was taken to the police station to be booked. Since this was his first felony arrest, the police did not have identification materials available on him. So, soon after entering the station house, Bill was fingerprinted, photographed, and asked for his address. Bill spent the rest of the night looking at the inside of the temporary holding cell in the police station.

On Tuesday morning, Bill was taken to a courtroom for a bail bond hearing. At the hearing, a judge said Bill could be released on bail until time to go to trial if he paid an amount of money. His bail was set at $5,000, but he was told only ten percent, or $500, was needed to post his bail and free him until the trial. Bill told the judge he had no money for bail or an attorney. Bill was returned to his temporary holding cell, and a public defender came to see him. Bill explained what he had done to his attorney, a public defender, who told Bill that he would go to court again the next day.

Wednesday, with the courts in full session, Bill was taken, along with his public defender, to a **preliminary hearing**. The judge heard the state's attorney present the evidence and decided there was reason to believe Bill may be guilty. Bill was then taken into another courtroom for arraignment where formal charges would be made against him. Since this was Bill's first arrest on any felony charge, his attorney explained that the charges against him would be read. His attorney further advised Bill that he would be required to plead guilty or not guilty.

Somewhat confused, and very scared, Bill asked what he should do. If he said he was not guilty, a jury trial would be ordered, he was told. If he were to plead guilty, he would not have a jury trial. Instead he would go before a judge for sentencing. Given the circumstances, he was advised by his attorney to plead guilty and let his attorney try to get a reduced sentence. Bill decided the advice was probably good, and he agreed to admit to the crime. When the arraignment was over, he was scheduled to appear before the circuit court judge a week later.

The following Wednesday, Bill was escorted to the circuit courtroom. Before he arrived, his lawyer (the public defender) had talked to the prosecutor (the state's attorney). When Bill arrived in court, his attorney explained that he had **plea bargained**, or made a deal with the state's attorney. Since Bill was going to plead guilty and it was his first offense, the state's attorney had agreed to ask the judge for a reduced sentence.

Soon, standing before the judge, Bill heard the charges read against him. Once more the judge asked if he were guilty as charged. Bill said, "Yes." Since Bill had fulfilled his part of the bargain, the state's attorney asked the judge for a reduced sentence. The judge agreed, and ordered a three-year **probation**. Bill's attorney explained that he would have to report, once each week, to a specially appointed officer of the court. This probation officer would help him find a job but would also check on him to make sure that Bill stayed out of trouble. If Bill failed to report regularly to his probation officer, he would most likely go to prison, he was told.

Now with a criminal court record and on probation, Bill could see that his quick money scheme had not been very wise. But at least he was not in prison, and someone would try to help find him a job, and maybe things would begin to improve.

Bill's story is a fairly simple one, but it shows the many checks in our court system. At each turn he was advised of his rights, given the opportunity of a jury trial, and finally given a reasonable punishment for his crime. If the case had gone to trial with Bill pleading not guilty, and if he were found guilty, Bill still would have the right to appeal the decision.

If Bill had been a minor, he would have gone through the Illinois juvenile court procedures. They are intended to be protective of children, even those who commit serious crimes. In all cases, whether a trial is conducted before a judge or jury, the purpose is the same — to enforce the laws of society and protect individual rights before the law. Remember, the key principle behind the federal and state judicial systems is that an individual is innocent until proven guilty. With that in mind, we have a system that does everything possible to protect the accused from wrongful conviction. ■

The officer arrests Bill and reads him his rights: He can remain silent; any answers he gives can be used against him in court; he can be represented by an attorney; and, if he can't afford an attorney, one will be provided free.

and judge. A chief judge is elected for each circuit by the circuit judges in that circuit. The chief judge is extremely important because he or she is in charge of seeing that all the cases move smoothly through the system.

The Appellate Courts

Most cases are settled at the circuit court level, but every citizen has the right to ask for another chance to be heard if the case was decided against him or her. The method to achieve another hearing is called an **appeal,** and the state court set up to hear appeals is the appellate court. It is the second of the three tiers.

Article VI, Sections 5 and 6 of the Illinois Constitution establishes the appellate court. The Constitution created five appellate court districts. Cook County, because of its large population compared to the rest of the state, was established as one district all by itself. The rest of the counties are divided into the other four districts, which are to be about the same in population.

Each appellate court may hold court anywhere within its district boundaries. The First District courtrooms are all in Chicago; the Second District meets in Elgin; the Third District has a court in Ottawa; the Fourth District sits in Springfield; and the Fifth District meets in Mt. Vernon. Normally, a case heard by an appellate court would have been tried in one of the circuit courts within its boundaries.

Like circuit court judges, appellate court judges are elected, but for terms of ten years. In 1997 there were 42 elected appellate court judges in Illinois. (Other appellate judges can be assigned or appointed by the Illinois Supreme Court.)

In some ways the appellate court system is simpler than the circuit court system. With five rather than 22 districts, the number of individuals needed to run the court is much smaller. The appellate court judges in each district appoint a clerk and other personnel as needed. Similar to the circuit court's chief judge, the appellate judges in each district pick a presiding judge to administer cases.

The circuit courts and appellate courts handle cases in different ways. At the circuit court level, a single judge hears the case, weighs the evidence, checks and interprets the laws that apply, and makes a decision, often aided by the use of a jury. If a case reaches the appellate court, only the lawyers are present, and the case is heard by a panel of three judges. In order for a decision to be made, two of the three appellate judges must agree.

The Illinois Supreme Court

Article VI of the state Constitution establishes the Illinois Supreme Court as the highest court in the state. The Constitution gives the Illinois Supreme Court original jurisdiction in a few instances, such as cases involving revenue (tax collection or expenditures). However, the Supreme Court, which meets both in Springfield and Chicago, is basically the highest appeals court in the state at the top of the three tiers.

Preliminary hearing A court hearing usually before a judge to determine if there is sufficient evidence to charge an individual with a crime.

Plea bargain An agreement in which a defendant pleads guilty, and the prosecutor in return agrees to a predetermined punishment, usually of lesser severity.

Probation The act of suspending the sentence of a person convicted of a criminal offense and granting that person freedom provided that he or she remains on good behavior.

Appeal The transfer of a case from a lower court to a higher court for the purpose of conducting a new hearing.

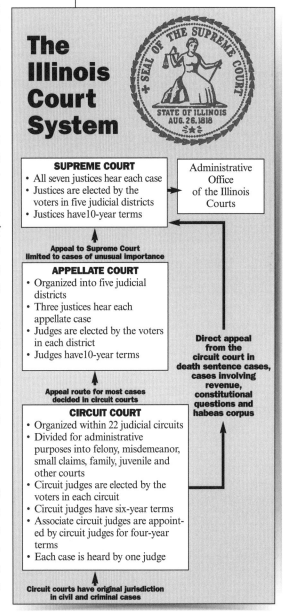

The Illinois Court System

SUPREME COURT
- All seven justices hear each case
- Justices are elected by the voters in five judicial districts
- Justices have 10-year terms

Administrative Office of the Illinois Courts

Appeal to Supreme Court limited to cases of unusual importance

APPELLATE COURT
- Organized into five judicial districts
- Three justices hear each appellate case
- Judges are elected by the voters in each district
- Judges have 10-year terms

Direct appeal from the circuit court in death sentence cases, cases involving revenue, constitutional questions and habeas corpus

Appeal route for most cases decided in circuit courts

CIRCUIT COURT
- Organized within 22 judicial circuits
- Divided for administrative purposes into felony, misdemeanor, small claims, family, juvenile and other courts
- Circuit judges are elected by the voters in each circuit
- Circuit judges have six-year terms
- Associate circuit judges are appointed by circuit judges for four-year terms
- Each case is heard by one judge

Circuit courts have original jurisdiction in civil and criminal cases

Unlike the appellate courts, which must accept all cases of appeal from the circuit courts, the Supreme Court has the right to decide which cases of appeal it will hear, with one exception: It must hear any case from the circuit court when the death penalty is imposed.

There are seven Illinois Supreme Court judges, called justices, and all seven hear and decide every case that comes before the Court. Whereas federal Supreme Court justices are appointed for life, Illinois elects its Supreme Court justices for terms of ten years. The five appellate court districts are also used for electing Supreme Court justices. Cook County elects three Supreme Court justices, and each of the other four districts elects one.

The Justices of the Illinois Supreme Court in January 1999: Justice Mary Ann G. McMorrow of Chicago; Justice James D. Heiple of Pekin; Justice Benjamin K. Miller of Springfield; Chief Justice Charles E. Freeman of Chicago; Justice Michael A. Bilandic of Chicago; Justice Moses W. Harrison II of Caseyville; and Justice S. Louis Rathje of Wheaton.

The three levels of courts are one unified system under the Supreme Court. Every three years the seven justices decide which one of them will be chief justice of the Illinois Supreme Court. The chief justice is responsible not only for administration of the Supreme Court, but also is in charge of the entire Illinois court system as well. The chief justice prepares a budget for operating the court system and makes sure that each court performs its constitutional duties.

The Power of the Judicial System

Most of the disputes that come before our state and federal courts deal with decisions based on the application of laws: Either the law was broken or improperly followed, or it was not. A small number of cases, however, involve constitutional issues. When the court decides issues of constitutionality, it is called **judicial review**. The power of judicial review is not spelled out in either the U.S. or Illinois constitutions. But, in a series of cases in the early nineteenth century, the U.S. Supreme Court established its power to review the constitutionality of laws made by the Congress. If a law is found to be in conflict with the U.S. Constitution, the U.S. Supreme Court may declare the law no longer in force. The Constitution of Illinois operates on this same basic idea, and the ultimate authority for deciding that state or local laws do not conflict with the Illinois Constitution rests with the

Illinois Supreme Court. In this way, the judiciary is a very powerful tool in assuring that the legislature passes no laws that violate its powers under the Constitution.

The Officers of the Judicial System

While the Illinois judicial system is established by the state Constitution, the actual function of the system involves many more individuals. We've already talked a little about judges when we looked at the three levels of the state judicial system. Now, let's take a look at:

- How judges are chosen
- Attorneys general and state's attorneys
- Other court employees
- The jury.

Choosing Our Judges

Every state has its own set of standards to become a judge. In Illinois, all judges must be licensed attorneys-at-law under Illinois regulations. They must be citizens of Illinois and live in the judicial area from which they are elected or appointed. Once an attorney becomes a judge, he or she may not carry on a private practice and must devote full time to court duties. In order to further avoid any conflicts of interest, anyone serving as a judge may not be elected to any other office. The judge is our most obvious and public link to the ideals expressed in our constitutions. Because of his or her position in the interpretation of law and the application of justice under those laws, the character and reputation of a judge must be beyond question.

One of the continuing controversies in Illinois is the method used to select our judges. To become a judge, an attorney must be nominated, campaign, and be elected. In order to remain a judge at the end of a term, the judge must run for retention of the office on the regular election ballot. Critics say that the system makes judgeships far too political, since the candidates are nominated in party primaries, and they run in the general election under a specific political party label. Supporters of the elective system say judges should be chosen by citizens because choosing them any other way could lead to control of the process by elite groups. Supporters say that both political parties reflect widely held attitudes. Critics argue that judges should hold their positions based on knowledge of the law, not on how well they campaign or on whether their party is the dominant one within the circuit or district. Critics contend that few voters know the judicial candidates or their qualifications, which defeats the purpose of the election process. When running for retention, the judge must receive three-fifths "yes" votes. Seldom, if ever, is the courtroom record of a judge discussed during a campaign, and voters often skip the retention question for a judge on ballots. Only a handful of judges in Illinois have failed to win retention.

Critics of electing judges have proposed that judges be appointed based on a system called merit selection. There are several variations of such systems used in other states. Generally, the governor would be given a list of qualified attorneys after a special commission has searched through their achievements and experience as lawyers. The governor would then appoint

In Illinois, all judges must be licensed attorneys-at-law under Illinois regulations. They must be citizens of Illinois and live in the judicial area from which they are elected or appointed. Once an attorney becomes a judge, he or she may not carry on a private practice and must devote full time to court duties.

the judges, usually to a specified term.

Those in favor of the elective system maintain it is the most democratic and representative method possible. Judges, because they are deciding cases, are in fact making law by interpreting it, and the people should have a voice to influence the law. Through election, they argue, judges are held accountable for their decisions: Good judges are kept, and bad ones rejected.

The only way to change the entire Illinois system of electing judges is by amending the state Constitution. A proposed amendment can be placed on the ballot by the General Assembly for the voters of Illinois to approve or reject. In 1970, when voters ratified the state Constitution, they were offered the separate question of appointing judges. The voters rejected the merit appointment of judges.

Attorney General and State's Attorney

The chief lawyer in Illinois is the attorney general. Elected statewide as a part of the executive branch, the attorney general is responsible for representing the state, or its officials, in lawsuits. He also advises the state's attorneys in the 102 Illinois counties.

One of the most important parts of the judicial system is the jury. The right to a trial by jury is guaranteed to citizens.

Section 19 of Article VI of the state Constitution requires that a state's attorney, sometimes also called a district attorney, be elected in each county. The state's attorney is exactly what the title implies, the attorney for the state in criminal and civil matters within a county. Since the state has its own attorney, anyone accused of a crime by the state has the right to be represented by an attorney also. Sometimes an individual cannot afford to hire an attorney, however, and the chief judge of the circuit court appoints a public defender. Most counties have regular public defenders. In less populous counties, the court will pay a private attorney to be a public defender.

Other Court Employees

In order to help the court run smoothly, several other people are important. To make a record of everything that is said in court the chief judge appoints a court reporter. Court reporters are present at all sessions of the Illinois courts.

Article VI, section 18 of the Illinois Constitution provides for the election or appointment of clerks to serve the circuit courts. The circuit clerk is responsible for keeping the records made by the reporters and any evidence

Illinois' system of courts, like those in all states, strive to interpret and carry out the law, while providing equal and fair protection to all citizens. Hearing mainly incidents of a civil or criminal character, cases may pass through three levels of the judiciary:

- Circuit courts
- Appellate courts
- The Illinois Supreme Court.

As a trial court, the circuit court is the first to hear cases and make decisions, deciding innocence or guilt. If people are not happy with the circuit court's decision, they may appeal the decision to an appellate court, which reviews the lower court's decision and decides if it was correct. Finally, if parties are still not satisfied they may appeal to the Illinois Supreme Court. The Supreme Court can decide which cases it reviews, but must hear appeals involving the death penalty.

The court system works because of the involvement of citizens. The officers of the courts — judges, attorney general, and state's attorney — are elected by the people, and juries are comprised of citizens just like you. ◼

💻 To find out more...
start with the *Governing Illinois* web site at **www.uis.edu/govern**

Petit jury A jury that sits at civil and criminal trials, usually consisting of 12 members.

Grand jury A jury of 12 to 23 people convened to evaluate accusations against people. The grand jury determines whether the evidence warrants charging suspects with a crime.

Indictment The act of formally charging someone with a crime or other offense.

submitted in a case. Since the organization of records is important, the circuit clerk appoints deputy clerks to serve in every courtroom in the circuit.

Even though the county sheriff is elected as a county — not circuit court — official, one of the sheriff's responsibilities is to help the circuit court. The sheriff and his or her deputies serve orders and warrants issued by the judges. To keep order and protect the judge, the sheriff appoints deputies to act as court bailiffs. Although appointed by the sheriff, the bailiff is an employee of the court.

The Jury

There are many more parts of the courts and judicial system that we could study. One of the most important is the jury. The right to a trial by jury is guaranteed to citizens. The Sixth Amendment of the U.S. Constitution says that "the accused shall enjoy the right to a speedy and public trial, by an impartial jury of the State and district wherein the crime shall have been committed." The Seventh Amendment guarantees the right to a jury in civil cases. The Illinois Constitution also ensures this right in Article I.

The jury at a trial is formally known as a **petit jury**, or small jury. In Illinois, the petit jury consists of twelve persons who have certain qualifications. Jurors must be at least eighteen years old and able to understand English. In addition they must be a resident and registered voter in Illinois. Jurors are called for service by a random selection from the list of registered voters and drivers.

The petit jury hears and decides both civil and criminal cases. Petit jurors normally serve for only one or two weeks at a time, but, if the trial continues beyond that time, jurors are required to remain until it is over. In Illinois, unanimous agreement by the jurors is needed for a conviction.

The other type of jury in Illinois is a **grand jury**. The grand jury consists of 23 people, chosen in the same way as a petit jury. The grand jury does not sit in a trial like a petit jury. The grand jury hears the state's attorney, also called the prosecutor, present evidence involving a crime. It is the grand jury that decides whether or not there is sufficient evidence to issue an **indictment**. Once an indictment, or a formal charge of a crime, has been issued, the individual is required to stand trial, and the normal trial sequence begins.

Although the grand jury is mentioned specifically in the U.S. Constitution, the Constitution does not require that a state call one. Illinois does use statewide grand juries, and Illinois has grand juries called by counties for serious violations of the law. Since the grand jury meets in secret to hear the prosecutor's evidence without the defendant or his attorney present, it can hear evidence not normally allowed in an open trial. Based on the information brought to it, the grand jury has the power to conduct its own investigation, calling witnesses and gathering evidence. Using information it receives in such a fashion, it can then issue a formal accusation of guilt if necessary. This method has been used effectively when dealing with underworld criminals, drug traffickers, white collar criminals, or corrupt government officials. The grand jury normally sits for thirty days, but it can sit as long as eighteen months. ◼

Chapter 7

Just because a government is local, doesn't mean it deals with small issues affecting few people. Decisions of the Chicago City Council and other metro-area local governments affect millions.

Illinois Local Government: Counties, Cities, Villages, Townships, Schools, and More

by Darlene Emmert Fisher and James M. Banovetz

It's a lovely spring day. You grab your skateboard and start out with your friends. After a few moments of skateboarding in a local parking lot, the village police show up.

Local governments The governments established to provide neighborhoods with public services, such as police, streets, parks, libraries, and schools.

Local government powers The authority — granted by the state — that allows a local government to do something, such as enforce traffic laws.

Home rule A constitutional right that gives Cook County and some cities the authority to determine, within limits, the powers they can exercise.

"You can't use those things here. It's against the village ordinances. Move on or we'll have to arrest you."

"Where can you use skateboards?" you ask.

"I don't know. The village council says no skateboarding on public property."

So what can you do? How can you find a place where you and your friends can skateboard?

Perhaps instead, on that lovely morning you go to the park to kick a soccer ball. But when you look around, you discover that so many dogs have been to the park already that there is no pleasant place to put your feet. What can you do about it?

Both situations are controlled by local government. So you need to approach local government in order to ease the restrictions on skateboarding or to write a pooper scooper law. **Local governments** are the governments closest to the people, operating at a neighborhood level to provide immediate services to people where they live. Every city and village is a local government. So is every county, township, park district, and school district. You turn to your local government to handle problems closest to you. Consider some of the basic functions of local government in your community:

- roads
- law enforcement
- education
- water and sewer services
- delivery of social and welfare services
- fire protection
- parks
- recreation programs
- waste disposal
- sanitation and health protection
- cemeteries, and more.

Local government is the part of government in which it is easiest for you to participate. You or a member of your family may be appointed to a committee; you may support a family friend who is a candidate for office; you may take part in efforts to influence the decision of the school board, the city council, or the county board; or some day you may even run for government office yourself. Because the other citizens involved in local government are your neighbors, it is easier to influence them and see the results of that influence than it is to influence the U.S. Congress or the state legislature.

The Power of Local Governments

There are four different kinds of local government in Illinois:

1. county governments,
2. municipal governments, which include cities and villages,
3. township governments, and
4. governments for special districts, such as school districts, park districts, and sanitary districts.

Later in the chapter we'll examine how these governments are set up and how they function. But first, let's talk about how **local government powers** come about.

Local governments have only those powers given them by the state. They can exercise only the functions specified for them in either the state Constitution or in state statutes. For most local governments, such powers are quite limited. They can get more powers only by going to the state legislature to ask for them.

Cook County and some municipalities have broader powers. These are given to them in the 1970 State of Illinois Constitution, Article VII, section 6. This section of the Constitution is called "Powers of Home Rule Units." A local government with **home rule** is more able to determine its own affairs. Governments that qualify for home rule powers can exercise any local powers not denied to them by state law or the Constitution, including making improvements to the roads and structures within their jurisdictions and assessing taxes to pay for those improvements.

Many municipalities have creatively used the power of home rule to attack their local problems. For example, Peoria used it to regulate people who sell food, such as hot dogs, from sidewalk carts. DeKalb used it to resolve disputes between landlords and Northern Illinois University students who rent apartments. Decatur used it to help finance the construction of a new hospital. Deerfield used it to pioneer a new way of controlling vandalism. And Oak Park used the power of home rule to help older residents maintain their homes. But the most common use of home-rule powers has been to help communities control their local economies and bring new jobs to town. Another common use has been to limit property tax increases by finding new taxes, such as taxes on the rental of hotel and motel rooms, restaurant meals, or theater and athletic tickets. These new taxes shift the burden of paying local taxes from residents to nonresident visitors.

All Illinois cities and villages with populations over 25,000 automatically have home rule unless voters specifically reject it in a referendum (a citywide vote). Smaller municipalities may adopt home rule by referendum. Counties acquire home-rule powers by providing for an elected chief executive officer. At the beginning of 1999, Cook County and over 140 municipalities had home rule.

Home rule is not unlimited. The Illinois Constitution curbs the powers that home-rule units employ, and it authorizes the General Assembly to do likewise. The drinking age problem inspired one limit to home rule powers. At one time, different communities used their home rule powers to establish different minimum drinking ages. Some set age nineteen; others set age twenty-one. Highway accidents increased as youths drove to communities where they could legally drink. Enforcing such a confused variety of laws became chaotic. Then, in 1980, the General Assembly passed a law making 21 the minimum drinking age for all of Illinois. The legislature's action meant that setting the drinking age was no longer a home-rule power.

Types of Local Government

According to the *1992 Census of Governments*, Illinois has over 6,700 units of local government, well more than any other state. Obviously, we can't describe each of these governments in this short chapter. But we will talk about each different kind of local government, and we'll give special attention to the city of Chicago and to Cook County. Census estimates from 1998 reflect that over 43 percent of the state's population lives in Cook County, which includes the city of Chicago, and the state has special regulations that apply only to Chicago and Cook County governments.

As we've noted before, there are four different kinds of local governments in Illinois:

1. county governments
2. municipal (city and village) governments
3. township governments
4. governments for special districts.

Counties are the basic unit of local government. All parts of the state are served by a county. Counties administer state services at the local level; they also provide many local services, especially in rural areas.

Municipal governments are the governments that oversee the operation of the state's cities, villages, and incorporated towns (all are also called municipalities). City and village governments are like counties in that they are **general purpose governments**. They are established to provide the broader range of local services required in urban areas.

Townships are found in eighty-five of Illinois' 102 counties. They provide a limited number of very local services. In Chicago and in the seventeen counties where townships do not exist, those functions are provided by county or municipal governments.

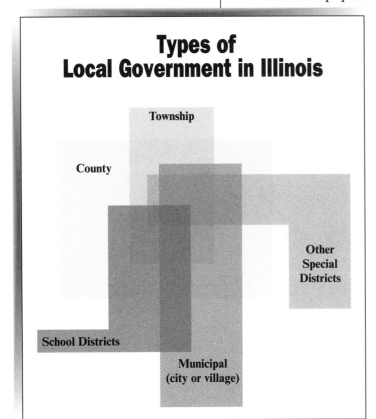

Types of Local Government in Illinois

Township

County

Other Special Districts

School Districts

Municipal (city or village)

The complexity of this diagram reflects the complexity of Illinois local government. Most neighborhoods in the state are served by a multitude of different governments, each with different purposes, responsibilities, and taxing powers. As shown in this figure, local governments don't even have common boundaries. Voters often have a hard time knowing which governments serve them.

Municipal governments The governments that cities, villages, and incorporated towns form to provide the higher level of public services needed by people who live in urban areas.

General purpose governments County and municipal governments charged by the state with the general responsibility to protect the "health, welfare, and safety" of the neighborhoods they serve. To do this, the state gives such governments a broad array of powers.

County governments The basic units of local government, they administer state services and provide local services in both rural and urban areas. County governments are general purpose local governments.

Special districts are governments formed to provide a single service to a particular geographic area. All public education in Illinois is provided by special districts (school districts). Other services often, but not always, provided by special districts include: parks (park districts), fire and ambulance services (fire protection districts), and sewage treatment (sanitary districts). The boundaries of such districts do not usually coincide with city, village, township, or county boundaries.

County Government

Illinois is divided into 102 counties. All parts of the state are located in one of these counties; all municipalities are located in one or more of these counties. (Some municipalities straddle county lines.)

County governments provide such services as law enforcement, roads, health protection, and welfare. Counties are also administrative subdivisions of the state, which means they administer elections; keep birth, death, and other vital records; and house the lowest level of the state's three-part court system, the circuit courts.

Each Illinois county has elected administrative officers. Under the Illinois Constitution, each county must elect a:

- **sheriff**, who is the county's chief law enforcement officer
- **clerk**, who administers elections and keeps the county's records
- **treasurer**, who is custodian of the county's money
- **state's attorney**, who prosecutes persons accused of crimes and is the county's chief legal officer.

Counties also elect a clerk of the circuit court, who maintains court records.

Counties have the option of electing a number of other officers, including a recorder to keep track of property records, an auditor to check the accuracy of county financial records, an assessor to calculate the value of taxable real estate, and a coroner to determine the cause of death of persons who die in accidents or under questionable circumstances.

Each county has a legislative body, called the **county board**, which makes county laws, called ordinances. Each also has an organized method to administer its services. But Illinois counties have different forms of governments, with different relationships between the county board and the administration of services.

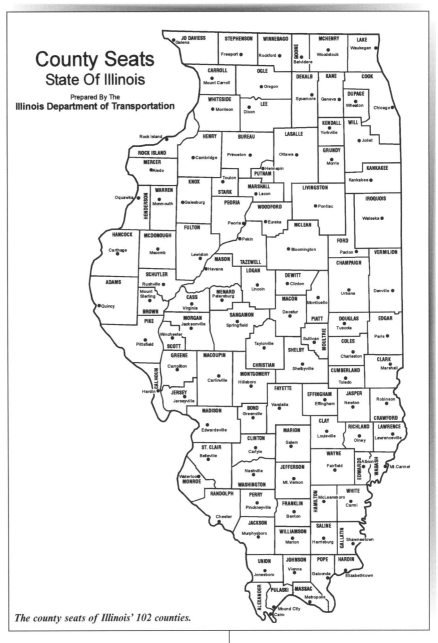

County Seats
State Of Illinois
Prepared By The
Illinois Department of Transportation

The county seats of Illinois' 102 counties.

Forms of County Government

The most common form of county government in Illinois is the county board. A county board is made up of members elected from districts within the county. (Boards generally have 15 to 29 members.) Board members elect one member to be the county board chair to run their meetings. Each board divides itself into committees, where most of the board's work is performed. Typically, there will be a separate board committee to supervise each of the administrative departments that report to the board.

Differing varieties of the county board form of government have

Sheriff The chief law enforcement officer (in other words, the police chief) in county governments.

Clerk A local government officer (found in both counties and municipalities) who helps administer elections and keeps the government's official records.

Treasurer A local government officer (found in both counties and municipalities) who collects and keeps safe the government's money.

State's attorney The lawyer for county government and also the lawyer who prosecutes people accused of crimes.

County board The county's legislative body, this is a group of elected officials who pass the county's laws and are responsible for seeing that the county provides services to the public.

evolved, and they can be categorized by how they organize themselves. For example, in DuPage county the county board chair is directly elected by the voters of the county. DuPage like many other county boards, has a position called the **county administrator**, someone the board hires to help manage important business and resolve important questions, such as helping prepare and manage the county budget and assisting in the supervision of administrative departments.

The second basic form of county government is the county commission. In this form, the voters elect a three-member board of commissioners who hold both the legislative and executive powers of the county. Typically, the position of board president is rotated among the commissioners. Each commissioner heads one of the county's administrative departments. Only the seventeen counties in southern Illinois that do not have township governments use this form of county government.

Illinois law also provides for a **county executive** form of government. This system is like the county board form except that all administrative power is in the hands of a county executive who is elected at-large by the voters of the county. Adoption of this form of government would give a county government home-rule powers, but to date no county has moved to adopt the county executive and accepted home-rule powers. State law also permits counties to adopt this form while rejecting home-rule powers for the county. Will County did this in 1988, and Kane County voters did the same in 1990.

Cook County Government

Cook County is unique. It is the only county specifically set forth in the state Constitution to have an elected chief executive officer and home-rule powers. Cook County has townships in its suburban areas, but it has no township government within the boundaries of the city of Chicago.

The Cook County Board is the legislative body of Cook County and the county board president is the chief executive officer. The board consists of seventeen members who are elected from single-member districts, having approximately 300,000 people. The board president has a special position because that person may be elected both as the president and separately as a commissioner. The president may vote as a commissioner and also veto as the president. The president's veto is unusually strong as a four-fifths vote of the board is required to override that veto. Terms of office for both board members and the president are four years, with election in even-numbered nonpresidential years.

Cook County also has other elected administrative officials: sheriff, county clerk, treasurer, assessor, state's attorney, recorder of deeds, and clerk of the court.

Township Government

In 84 of Illinois' 102 counties, the land within the county is subdivided into townships, each of which has its own **township government.** The township is grass-roots government, the government closest to the people in rural areas. The township is also a basic unit for political party

County administrator A professional trained and experienced in local government management who is hired by the county board to assist it in directing the daily operations of county government.

County executive An elected official who chairs county board meetings and manages the daily operations of county government.

Township governments Local governments, found in 84 Illinois counties, which provide a very limited number of local services and duties.

Township supervisor An elected official who chairs township board meetings and manages the daily operations of township government, including the administration of the township's poor relief program.

Assessor A person who places a monetary value on land and buildings for property tax purposes. Depending on the form of government, assessors may be either county or township officials and may be either elected or appointed.

Forms of County Government in Illinois

County Governments

County Board Forms of Government[1]

County Commission Form of Government[2]

County Executive Form of Government[3]

Cook County Government

County board is elected by the people. The board members elect a president among themselves.

County board is elected by the people. The president of the county board is also elected by the people.

County board is elected by the people. The county board hires an administrative officer to help manage its business.

The people elect a three-member board of commissioners who usually rotate the presidency among themselves.

Like the county board form of government, except that all administrative power is in the hands of one executive.

The county is divided into districts. People in the county elect a county board commissioner from their district. The county board president must be elected by the people of the county as president and may also be elected by the people of his or her district as a commissioner.

[1] County board members are elected from districts with one or more members elected per district.

[2] County commissioners are elected at large.

[3] County board members currently are elected from single-member districts.

organization in Illinois.

Elected township officials include the members of the board of trustees, the **township supervisor**, an **assessor**, and a collector. These officers are elected for four-year terms.

Townships have three primary functions. They:

1. develop and maintain township roads
2. deliver help to the needy
3. assess the value of local property for tax purposes.

Through the supervisor, the township may also provide other social services, such as child care, job training, youth programs, senior citizen programs, housing improvement, and health care, which may include a drug abuse program. These social services have become increasingly important in the townships surrounding Chicago.

Municipal Government and its Forms

According to the *1992 Census of Governments*, Illinois leads the nation with 1,282 municipal governments. Almost 85 percent of Illinoisans live in areas governed by municipal governments. Municipalities are also called cities, villages, and incorporated towns. (Do not confuse an incorporated town with township government.) Municipalities are independent government structures; they are not a part of either the county or township governments that serve the same area. Municipalities are usually formed when local residents petition the state to establish a city, a village, or an incorporated town because they want more services than those provided by counties and townships. Such services could include city water and sewer systems.

Municipalities are located where people needed them; they were not set up by any master plan. Each established municipality has had its own reason or reasons for attracting people — a good river or lake port, a good rail location for shipping grain or other goods, a college, a bustling crossroads with stores and services set up to supply farmers who had settled on Illinois' rich prairie land. There are other reasons today, but all have to do with earning a good living. Municipal governments were established to help serve the people attracted to these places.

There are several forms of city government possible in Illinois. Among them are:

1. the aldermanic form of government
2. the city manager form of government
3. the commission form of government
4. the strong-mayor form of government.

Each of these forms of government provides for an elected mayor and legislative body, called either a **city council** or a commission, depending upon the form. Each also provides for a city clerk or city treasurer. But whether these officials are elected or appointed is determined either by the form of government or by local preference. Each form of city government has its own advantages and disadvantages.

The Aldermanic Form of City Government

The vast majority of Illinois' cities have an aldermanic form of government. Also called the "weak mayor-council form," it works well in smaller municipalities. It is called weak mayor-council because, under state law, the mayor's administrative powers are shared with the council. Of course, that

Forms of City Government in Illinois

City Governments

The Aldermanic Form (Also called the Weak Mayor-Council Form)	The City Manager Form	The Commission Form	The Strong-Mayor Form
• The elected mayor shares administrative powers with the members of the city council (or aldermen). • Aldermen are elected from districts (or wards). • Cities may use either single-member districts or elect two aldermen per district. • The city clerk and city treasurer may be either elected at large or appointed by the mayor and council.	• Voters elect a mayor and a city council. • City council members can be elected at large, from a district, or from a combination of at large and districts. • The mayor and the council hire a manager to run the day-to-day operations of the city. • The city clerk and the city treasurer may be elected at large or appointed by the mayor and council.	• The voters elect a mayor and four commissioners. • The mayor and commissioners are elected at large. • Each commissioner is in charge of one or more of the functions of city government, such as finance or public works. • A city clerk and a city treasurer are appointed.	• The mayor is elected at large and is the chief executive in charge of all the city's administrative departments. • Members of the city council are elected from districts. • The city council makes policy and passes ordinances. • The city clerk and the city treasurer may be elected at large or appointed by the mayor and council.

doesn't mean that the **mayor** may not be a strong personality with great leadership ability. A succession of Chicago mayors, such as Richard J. Daley, Harold Washington, and Richard M. Daley, illustrates that the term "weak mayor" is organizational, not personal. In fact, many of the aldermanic communities throughout the state elect mayors who are strong political and governmental leaders.

These cities are known as aldermanic because the members of their city councils — their legislative bodies — are elected from wards, or districts, within the city. These ward representatives are called aldermen (whether or not they are men or women). Sometimes two aldermen are elected from each district; in other cities, only one is elected per district. In most cities, the aldermen serve a four-year term of office; in a few cities, the term of office is only two years. The council makes policy, passes ordinances, and decides how the city's services will be managed.

City council members elected under the aldermanic form of city government represent wards, or districts, within the city.

The City Manager Form of City Government

The city manager form is like the aldermanic form. Voters elect a mayor and members of the city council. The council members may be elected from wards or districts within the city; they may be elected at large (citywide); or some council members may be elected at large while others are elected from wards. The terms of office and voting powers of the mayor and council members are the same as those in the aldermanic form.

The unique part of this form of city government is that the mayor and council hire a **city manager**, a professional administrator with training and experience in managing city business. The mayor and council, together, hire the person they feel is best suited to meet the needs of the city. The city manager does not have a specified term of office or appointment. Instead, the manager serves at the pleasure of the council and can be fired whenever the council feels that a change is needed.

In this form of city government, the mayor and the council together have all of the legislative power to pass ordinances, make city policy, levy taxes, approve the city's budget, and hire and fire the manager.

The manager, in turn, directs the daily operation of the city's government. He or she:
- hires, supervises, and fires department heads, such as the police chief and the public works director
- manages the city's expenditures to keep costs as low as possible
- directs all efforts made to carry out the council's policies for the city
- accepts accountability to the council for the work of all city employees.

City council The legislative body of a city. The council makes the city's policies, passes local laws, approves the city's annual budget, and helps direct the city's daily operations.

Mayor The chief elected official of a city. The mayor's duties include chairing the meetings of the city council and providing leadership in making city policies. In some cities, the mayor also plays a leading role in managing the daily affairs of the city government. Some villages also use this term informally when referring to the village president, the village's chief elected official.

City manager A professional administrator with specific training and experience in the management of local governments. A city manager is hired by the city council, not elected to office.

City administrator An appointed official who manages the daily operations of city government. A city administrator performs the same function as a city manager, but does so in a city that does not operate under the city manager form of government.

Strong-mayor form of government A system of municipal government in which the mayor is given major responsibility, usually by state law, for administering the daily operations of city government. This is in contrast to the weak-mayor systems found in most Illinois cities where the mayor either has no authority to administer daily operations or has only the authority gained from the role of leader and chair of the city council.

Village president An elected official whose duties in the village are the same as the duties of the mayor of a city. Many village presidents are informally called "mayor."

Village board The legislative body of village government that performs the same duties in the village as city councils do in cities. The members of the village board are elected to office.

Village administrator A professional local government manager who is hired by a village board to manage the daily business and activities of the village government and to advise the village board on policy matters.

It is the manager, for example, who must see that the city's water is safe to drink, that the parks are clean, that laws against the sale of illegal drugs are enforced, and that the streets are kept in good repair. The manager also serves as an adviser to the council on needed changes in public policies. Most of Illinois' larger Chicago suburbs and the larger cities downstate now use the city manager form of government.

An increasing number of Illinois cities organized under the aldermanic form of government are now employing a city manager to serve as the city's chief administrative officer and help the council manage the daily business of government. These cities often call this officer the **city administrator**. While the job duties of city administrators are usually similar to those of city managers, the actual duties of such an officer are spelled out in an ordinance adopted by the city employing him or her.

The Commission Form of City Government

In this form of government, voters elect a mayor and four commissioners on an at large basis. Together, these five people serve as the legislative body for local lawmaking. Each commissioner also is the administrative head of one of the city's departments, such as finance or public works. The council appoints a clerk and a treasurer. Once very popular, the commission form of government is now used in only 28 of the 408 Illinois cities and villages with populations over 2,500. Many people consider this form obsolete.

In the late 1980s, in both Springfield and Danville the federal courts threw out the commission form of government because the at large elections never resulted in election of an African-American commissioner. To guarantee representation of this minority of citizens, these cities now elect council members from wards or districts.

The Strong-Mayor Form of City Government

Illinois law permits cities to choose a **strong-mayor form of government** In this form, the mayor, by law, becomes the chief executive officer in charge of the work of all the administrative departments. The council's role is to make policy and pass ordinances. In this form, too, the mayor may appoint a professional administrator to help supervise city employees. No Illinois city has adopted this option by vote of the people in a referendum, but at least three Illinois cities use a modified version of the strong-mayor form. Rockford and Aurora adopted many elements by ordinance; Springfield adopted this form in response to a court mandate that it drop the commission form.

Village Government

The village form of municipal government provides for the election of a **village president** (often informally called the mayor) and a legislative body called the village board of trustees, or just the **village board**. Such boards usually have six members called trustees. Villages also have a village clerk and village treasurer; as in cities, these officials may be elected or appointed depending on local preference.

Nearly all villages in Illinois elect members of the village board at large rather than from wards. The powers and duties of the village president and the village board are essentially the same as those of the mayor and city council in cities operating under the aldermanic form of city government.

Villages may also, by law, adopt the city manager form of government. When they do so, the city manager is called the village manager. Alternately, like cities with the aldermanic form of government, villages may hire a professional administrator, called the **village administrator**, to manage their daily activities.

Many people think of cities as large governments and villages as small governments, but there is no law that says so. The village of Skokie, for example, with a 1990 census population of 59,432 likes to advertise itself as "the world's largest village." The city of Leland Grove

Chicago City Government

The government of the city of Chicago is based on the weak mayor-council model. The elected officials include the mayor, who is elected at large, and a city council consisting of aldermen elected from 50 wards (one per ward). The city clerk and treasurer are also elected.

The mayor is the chief executive officer who appoints administrative staff for the city's operating departments and for the 24 boards and commissions funded directly by the city. Chicago has more than one hundred boards, commissions, and advisory groups. Most of their members are appointed by the mayor and approved by the council. This includes members of the boards of otherwise independent agencies, such as the Board of Education, the City Colleges, the Chicago Housing Authority, and the Chicago Transit Authority. The mayor presides at city council meetings and can vote in the case of a tie. The mayor must approve or veto all ordinances passed by the city council. It is the Democratic Party primary that usually determines who will be Chicago's mayor because the winner of

Richard J. Daley was mayor of Chicago from 1955 to 1976. His son, Richard M. Daley won election to his first term as mayor in 1989.

the Democratic primary has won every mayoral election for the past 70 years.

Each alderman on the Chicago city council represents a ward of about 60,000 people and serves a four-year term. Aldermen are elected on a nonpartisan ballot at the same time as the mayoral primary (in February). If no candidate receives a majority in the regular election in a particular ward, there is a runoff election in April between the two candidates with the most votes. Even though the aldermanic elections have nonpartisan ballots, most people know to which political party the candidates belong.

An alderman may or may not also be a ward committeeman. Each ward may have two committeemen — one Republican and one Democrat — who represent their party in the ward. The position of committeeman is an unpaid, elective party office separate from the aldermanic position, yet often the Democratic committeeman is very influential in Chicago's city government. ■

had 1,679 people according to the 1990 census.

Special Districts

According to the *1992 Census of Governments*, Illinois has 2,920 special district governments. Once you become a property tax payer, you will become aware of these special districts because they show up on your property tax bill. Each levies its separate tax within its district boundaries.

Each **special district** deals with a particular problem and provides a particular public service. Why does Illinois have so many of them? Some were created to provide services on a regional basis; others to provide services that existing governments could not afford. Still others were established to provide services that existing local governments could not provide. County governments, for example, are not permitted by state law to have fire departments. Thus, many people in rural areas established special fire protection districts.

The largest number of special districts are for drainage and flood control, fire protection, parks and recreation, and sewage. All of these districts serve important purposes, yet there are problems. Boundary lines are rarely the same for different kinds of governments serving the same area. Responsibility for local services is divided among so many boards that citizens become confused. As a result, citizens do not understand which government does what, and they frequently blame their city or county governments for tax increases imposed by the boards of special districts. Also, because of this confusion, special district boards often can and do raise taxes free of public resistance. The final result of so many special districts can be high local property taxes.

Because there are so many special districts, citizens in Illinois have a greater opportunity to take part in local government than citizens in most other states. Each special district has its own governing board made up of local citizens. In some districts, these board members are elected; in others they are appointed by the local city council or county board. Usually, each special district board appoints a chief executive officer to oversee the day-to-day functions of the district in much the same manner the city manager does in a city.

Funding for the construction and maintenance of park and recreation facilities — such as the Lake County Forest Preserves' bike trail — are the responsibility of park districts. A park district is just one of many kinds of local-level special districts found throughout Illinois.

School Districts — The Most Famous Special Districts

Of all the special districts, the best known are for schools. According to 1997-1998 figures from the Illinois State Board of Education, there are 899 public school districts in Illinois.

Illinois has four types of school districts:

1. Unit districts that oversee schools for kindergartners through 12th-graders
2. Elementary districts that have only elementary and middle or junior high schools
3. Secondary districts have only high schools
4. Community college districts.

Because there are so many districts, the state encourages consolidation, which is the combining of two or more districts into one.

Every **school district** (except Chicago) elects citizens to serve as the **school board**. The board sets policy for its schools on curriculum and textbooks, hires and fires the **school superintendent**, establishes the school budget, and levies local property taxes to help pay for schools. The superintendent is the chief administrative officer. He or she is responsible for hiring teachers and other staff, supervising the educational programs, and carrying out the policy decisions made by the school board within the general requirements of state law. Federal law also influences local school board decisions.

The Chicago Public Schools

Chicago's public schools are the only public schools in Illinois that are not operated by an independently elected school district. Chicago's schools are operated by a school board whose members are appointed by the mayor of Chicago and approved by Chicago's city council.

In decades past, the Chicago school system was plagued by labor strife between the Chicago Teachers Union and the Chicago School Board and school administration. Such strife led to teachers' strikes almost every year and resulted in chronic budget deficits. By 1995, fed up with these problems and reports of poor performance by Chicago's students, the General Assembly acted to centralize responsibility for Chicago's schools directly in the office of the mayor.

Chicago Mayor Richard M. Daley responded by abolishing the office of school superintendent. He replaced the superintendent with a management team headed by Chief Executive Officer Paul Vallas, a professional administrator but not a professional educator. Under this new leadership, the Chicago public education system experienced substantial reforms, some of which produced the first balanced budget in more than 20 years, and others that resulted in increased student performance as measured by standardized tests.

Chicago Mayor Richard M. Daley named Paul Vallas as the chief executive officer of Chicago's public schools after the General Assembly acted to centralize responsibility for schools directly in the office of the mayor in 1995.

Another unique feature of Chicago's schools, one also added in an effort to improve the performance of the city's schools, has been the creation of a local school council for each of the city's public schools. These councils, made up of elected representatives who are parents, instructional and administrative staff members, and, sometimes, students, select their

Special districts Special governments formed to provide a particular service to the region that they serve. In Illinois, all public schools are provided for by special districts called school districts.

School district A special district unit of local government that is organized to provide public education.

School board The school district's legislative body. Members of the school board are elected to office. A school board makes school and educational policy for the district, approves the school budget, levies property taxes to support the schools, and hires a school superintendent to manage the daily operation of the educational program.

School superintendent The chief operating officer of the school district. A professional educator and administrator, the school superintendent hires the school district's teachers and administrative staff, prepares and manages its budget, and oversees the operation of the educational program.

school's principal and play an instumental role in shaping the school's education program.

Overlapping Local Governments — Figuring Out Who's in Charge

As we've seen, there are many forms of local governments in Illinois. If all this government is confusing to you at first, don't worry. The complexities of local government can be confusing to everyone including, sometimes, the very people who serve in local government.

When there is a problem in your community, finding out exactly who is responsible for creating it (or for fixing it) can be difficult. Especially complicated are the decision-making relationships between governments serving the same geographic area, such as townships, villages, counties, and school districts. For example, people living in the city of DeKalb are served by the city, by DeKalb County, by the DeKalb Unit School District, by DeKalb Township, by the DeKalb Park Board, by a community college board, by the DeKalb Sanitary District. The boundaries of all of these governments are not the same. The school district boundaries include land outside the city limits; the city's boundaries include DeKalb Township, but also part of several other townships.

This overlapping of governments in one geographic area leads to questions about who is responsible for providing what service. For example who provides police protection to a school district with borders overlapping county and village boundaries? Does the city health department have control of the way food is served in the school district cafeteria?

Sometimes such disputes over government responsibility have to be settled in court. But, more often, the confusion is settled without involving the judicial system, and public policy decisions are made through long, time-consuming processes of negotiation among the governments involved, private citizens with a special interest in the matter, affected interest groups, and sometimes agencies of federal and state governments. Sometimes this confusion gets a little comical. The city of DeKalb is served by four law enforcement agencies: the city police, the county sheriff's department, the Northern Illinois University campus police, and the State Police. One day, when students blocked a state highway in the middle of a campus demonstration, the four police departments met in the middle of the street and argued about which department was in charge and responsible for dealing with the students.

Whether the situations are comical or confusing, much of the work of local government, and indeed much of the work of all governments, is accomplished through different government agencies working together. When many different governments work together to solve a problem, the process is called **intergovernmental relations**. An example of this process is provided in the case study presented at the conclusion of chapter 2.

Influences on Local Government

Everyone has an interest in influencing local government because local government affects everyone where they live. Local government tries to solve our everyday problems, including broken streetlights, potholes, or the need for a plan to get rid of garbage. People who call their city's alderman or their county board member with a complaint can be influencing government decisions. Government decisions are also influenced by citizen interest groups who pressure city councils, county boards, and other local government officials through organized campaigns.

It's often difficult to reach those who serve in the state and federal government, but the decision-makers of local government are easy to reach, and citizens have a greater chance to influence them, especially if they organize.

Not only do local citizens reach up to influence their local governments, but higher levels of government reach down to influence local affairs. Funds provided by state and federal grants for particular services, such as welfare or roads, make a difference in local decision-making.

The Influence of Interest Groups on Local Government

Interest groups try to influence the decisions of every kind and form of local government. Such groups include a chamber of commerce looking for favorable business conditions, such as better parking for customers. They include neighborhood groups seeking to improve parks or police protection or the enforcement of building codes. They include taxpayer groups concerned about high taxes and humanitarian groups trying to have government solve homelessness. And they include citizens like you looking for a place to skateboard.

Interest groups may be small and informal or large and very well-organized. People may band together to deal with one special problem, such as the need for a traffic light at a busy intersection. Once the local government responds to that problem, this type of group may dissolve. Another group formed to see that the local park is kept clean may continue as a group for years to keep the pressure constantly on government. Even small, informal groups can exert a major influence on a local government.

Political parties may also have major influence on local government, but many municipalities have sought to reduce the pressures of national and state politics on local matters through nonpartisan elections. In a nonpartisan election, candidates for mayor or alderman are not listed with a party label on the voting ballot. The candidates may or may not be members of the Democratic or Republican parties, but they are not officially identified with either label for the local election. Sometimes citizens will develop local parties with names such as Citizen's Caucus or Citizen's Party in order to find and support qualified candidates for local government offices. Such local parties may be listed on ballots in some communities.

In general, national political parties, Republican or Democratic, do not have much influence on local Illinois governments except in some of the largest cities, counties, and townships. Most municipalities, schools, and other special districts operate with little party influence and with people appointed to government jobs on the basis of merit rather than party activity.

The Influence of Media on Local Government

Another powerful influence on local government is the local media. If there is a local newspaper, television, or radio station, the opinions of the people controlling those media are very important to government. Because there are often few sources of information in most communities, the news of a village council as reported (or not reported) by a local newspaper or radio station makes a big difference in the way people think about the council's decisions.

If, for example, the local newspaper reports that garbage is piling up in backyards and the council is ignoring the problem, the citizens will probably become angry. If a particular local business is given a contract to provide supplies for city hall and no other businesses are allowed to compete for the business, the news media should report this unfairness to the public. If no one asks or reports the situation to the community, nothing will change. The media play a major role in keeping people informed and in influencing the opinion people have of their government.

Citizens must be careful, however, not to rely solely on the local news media for information about government. Members of the media can and do make mistakes; information in the newspaper or on the radio or TV can be wrong. Sometimes the media fail to report stories. For example, what if the business that got the no-bid city contract in the above example is an advertiser in the newspaper? It's possible that the publisher of the local paper would choose not to report the apparent unfairness of the city council's action. Thus, citizens need always to remain alert for information about their governments.

Local media are powerful influences on local government. The news of a village council, city council, or county board as reported by a local paper makes a big difference in the way people think about their local governments.

Referendum An election in which voters decide an issue of public policy, such as whether to provide money to build more schools or whether to change a city's form of government.

Developers Business people who finance and create new uses for land and buildings. They invest money and effort into attempts to change land uses. They hope that their effort will make the land and buildings more useful to the community, thereby creating a profit for themselves and their investors.

The Voters' Influence on Local Government

The citizens themselves are an important influence on any local government. As voters, they elect government leaders, and they may refuse to reelect officeholders who have not been sensitive to their wishes.

There are also times when the elected representatives, such as the members of a city council or school board, do not have the power to make decisions for the people. Instead, all the voters get to help make the decision by voting in a **referendum**. A referendum may be required for increasing taxes, going into debt, changing the form of government,

A Modern Problem and Pressure: Developers

In recent years certain business men and women called **developers** have become major interest groups pressuring municipalities and counties of every size. Developers are in the business of changing the use of large parcels of land. Developers, for example, might buy farmland and build housing on it, or they might tear down old, outmoded factories and use the sites to build modern commercial or industrial buildings. Their plans for land and buildings are called developments.

Developers need local government help to provide public services such as water, sewer, and police and fire protection for their new developments. They also need

Developments can bring more jobs, more tax revenue, and attractive new buildings to a community. But they can also bring increased traffic, strain municipal services budgets, and reduce the amount of open space in a community.

cooperation on such city regulations as parking, land use, construction permits, or taxation. Because the developers want to make a profit from their finished developments, they will try very hard to get governments to provide such services and to cooperate on local regulations.

Developers try to convince officials of the good things their development will bring to the community; more jobs, more tax revenue for government services, and attractive new or renovated facilities. Developments are often opposed, however, because they can increase traffic, put pressure on municipal services, reduce the amount of open

space, cause architecturally interesting and historic buildings to be torn down, or cause pollution.

The arguments can be intense, making it hard for local officials to decide what is best.

Developers are often far better organized and prepared with information than either local governments or citizens' groups.

Developers as a special interest group are growing in influence. Some local governments, especially in rapidly expanding areas, face decisions on developments every day. Other communities have little to attract developers and might actually welcome the challenge of dealing with them. ∎

or getting (or getting rid of) home rule. All these referenda are binding, meaning the decision of the voters must be followed. There are also advisory or nonbinding referenda that let local officials know how the citizens feel about an issue.

Economic Pressures and Their Influence on Local Government

Economic pressures influence the decisions of local government. Remember that people move or stay because of jobs. Some Illinois communities, especially those in counties surrounding Chicago, are experiencing

SUM IT UP

Local government is the level of government that most affects you, the citizen. It is your local government that operates your school; provides your parks, recreation programs, and swimming pools; fixes your roads and streets; fights crime and keeps your neighborhood safe; puts out fires and rescues people in danger; runs your emergency ambulance service; provides welfare and many other social services; controls the quality of new real estate developments; imposes zoning on property to protect your neighborhood and the value of your home; and, yes, imposes taxes on your house or apartment to pay for such services. If you live in a city or a village, your local government probably also provides your home with clean, healthy water; collects and cleans your sewage; and picks up, recycles or otherwise disposes of your garbage.

Local governments can only exercise the functions given to them in either the Constitution or by state laws. Each is thus limited in the services it can perform, the rules it can make, and the taxes it can impose. But Cook County and some municipalities have broader, home-rule powers that allow them to exercise any local powers not denied to them by state law or the Constitution.

There are four types of local government in Illinois:

1. County government
2. Township government
3. Municipal government
4. Special districts.

The powers and responsibilities of these governments — as well as the geographic areas they serve — sometimes overlap. So, sometimes it's difficult to figure out who is responsible for what. Who pays for repaving Oldham Road? The city council? The county board? What if the road goes through Oldham Park? Maybe the park district is responsible for the road's upkeep? Resolving these questions takes persistence on the part of citizens and, maybe, intergovernmental relations on the part of the overlapping governmental structures.

There are three basic types of county government in Illinois:

1. The county board type, made up of members elected from districts within the county.
2. The county commission form, in which voters elect a three-member board of commissioners who hold both the legislative and executive powers of the county.
3. A county executive form of government, which is like the county board form except that all administrative power is in the hands of a county executive who is elected at large by the voters of the county.

In 84 of Illinois' 102 counties, the land within the county is subdivided into townships, each of which has its own government. Townships have three primary functions. They:

1. Develop and maintain township roads
2. Deliver help to the needy
3. Assess the value of local property for tax purposes.

Four different types of municipal (city or village) governments operate in Illinois. They are:

1. The aldermanic form
2. The city manager form
3. The commission form
4. The strong-mayor form.

The type of city government determines how the city council is elected, how government is managed, and whether the city government must hire a professional administrator to manage the business of the city or village.

Illinois is filled with special districts that provide particular public services (e.g. schools, parks, sewage) or deal with a specific problem. These districts also levy property taxes to pay for the services they provide.

Local governments pay attention to the influences exerted on them by:

• Special interest groups
• Media
• Economic pressures
• Voters, and
• People like you.

Because local governments are made up of your neighbors, you have more opportunity to participate and influence the workings of your local government than you have to influence the workings of the state and federal government. ■

rapid growth. Business is booming and people are moving there. Governments there must deal with needs for new facilities for water, sewage, transportation, recreation, and local shopping. For other communities in Illinois, growth has slowed or stopped altogether because their major industries have gotten into trouble. Governments in such cities as Rock Island, Peoria, Decatur, and Cairo must deal with ways of attracting new jobs or helping their existing businesses expand. ■

To find out more...
start with the *Governing Illinois* web site at **www.uis.edu/govern**

Chapter 8

While riding down the escalator at your favorite mall, taxes are probably the last thing on your mind. But the fact is, taxes are everywhere.

The Way it Works: State Finances

by Michael D. Klemens

I t's one of those blustery March days that isn't good for much. It's too muddy to play ball and too cold to hang around the park. Your dad or your mom is sitting at the kitchen table with a calculator and a stack of papers barking orders about this receipt or that check and complaining about taxes. "I'm doing the taxes," you're told. It does not look fun.

Clearly it's not a day to hang around the house. So you call up Eddie — he's got his driver's license and his mom lets him take the car — and propose a trip to the mall. Anything to get away from those taxes.

As of now, there is no sales tax on tickets to the movies in most Illinois communities. Nor is there a tax on what you pay a barber or a beautician, a lawyer, or a doctor.

Taxes Money the government collects from its citizens to provide services.

Motor fuel or gasoline taxes State and/or local taxes charged on each gallon of gasoline a driver buys.

Bonds A way for a government (or a business) to borrow money. Governments sell bonds, which are promises to pay a specific amount of money at a specific time in the future. Investors buy bonds because at maturity (the date when the government buys back the bonds) the bonds are worth more than their original sales price.

Sales taxes Taxes imposed by state and local governments on the purchase of goods.

Taxes Are Everywhere

Where does your parents' tax money go and why do they need to pay those taxes? The simple answer is that **taxes** are legislated contributions that people and corporations pay to the government. Government today — whether it be the national government in Washington, D.C., Illinois' state government in Springfield, or one of the local governments serving your community — is a big and complex business. Governments have to deal with many problems. All the services that the government provides involve spending money. One of the ways a government gets the money it needs to provide services and solve problems is to levy taxes on the people it governs.

You may think of yourself as just a poor student. Maybe you don't even have a job outside your home. But you can't get away from taxes. Everybody pays them, even teenagers who hang around the mall on early spring Saturdays. Let's keep an eye on the taxes paid in an afternoon at the mall.

Eddie arrives 45 minutes after your call with Rob and Jeff in tow. "Hey guys, I need gas. Ante up," he says.

Gas is $1.29 cents a gallon, so a dollar apiece buys you a little over three gallons. About 35 cents of each dollar goes for taxes. Actually, four dollars gets you $2.60 worth of gasoline and pays $1.40 in taxes to the federal, state, and local governments.

Taxes on Gasoline

When you buy gasoline in Illinois you pay two different kinds of state taxes, **gasoline taxes** (the precise name is **motor fuel taxes**) and sales taxes. To those who pay them, a tax is a tax; the difference comes in how the taxes are used. Motorists pay gasoline taxes on each gallon of gasoline they buy. The state uses some of this tax money to build and maintain highways. The state highway crew you see patching the road is probably paid with gasoline tax money. So is the crew building the new relief highway around the city, but less directly. When building new roads the state usually borrows the money to build the road by selling **bonds**, and then pays the money back to the bondholders with money raised from gasoline taxes. Finally, Illinois shares some of the money from its gasoline tax with local governments (cities, villages, counties, and townships). The local governments use their portion to build new roads, fix potholes, and paint stripes on the highways.

In addition to gasoline taxes, most Illinoisans also pay local gasoline taxes. In early 1999, the total local gasoline taxes in Chicago were 11 cents per gallon. In Cook County outside Chicago they were six cents per gallon. In DuPage County they were four cents per gallon. Eighteen other cities and two counties have imposed gasoline taxes, ranging from five cents to a half cent per gallon.

The other tax that you pay when you buy gasoline in Illinois is the sales tax. **Sales taxes** are charged for the purchase of goods. When you buy a dollar's worth of gasoline, you will pay state sales taxes of six cents. You will pay some local sales taxes, too, in most places in Illinois. Local sales taxes, for example, help pay the cost of operating mass transit systems in and around Chicago.

Although a tax is a tax, the difference between gasoline and sales taxes is how they are spent. The state sales tax is the second largest source of money that the state uses for general operating expenses. That means the sales tax is used for things like running schools and public universities, operating prisons, paying welfare grants, providing mental health hospitals, and investigating child abuse.

That is a long-winded explanation. As you pump your four dollars' worth into the tank, the numbers just flash forward on the pump, without distinguishing between the price of gasoline and the taxes on gasoline.

Sales Taxes

You arrive at the mall and inside is an auto show. New car dealers are showing their wares. A Porsche catches your eye. Price: $45,200 plus tax. Rob growls that he could probably buy a used car with the tax on the Porsche. He's right. The total sales tax on the Porsche would be nearly $2,825. And then he would have to pay to register the car (buy license plates), a $78 charge that would seem pretty insignificant on a new car.

Buy a pair of shoes or a new t-shirt, and you'll pay sales tax.

More taxes. It's enough to make a guy thirsty. Run in and buy a soda, and you'll run into more taxes. You're going to pay sales tax on that soda, a burger, or french fries. Buy a pair of shoes or a new t-shirt, and you'll pay sales tax. How about the newest CD from your favorite rock group? More sales taxes.

Is nothing sacred? Is there no place to escape taxes? You could go watch a movie. As of now, there is no sales tax on tickets to the movies in most Illinois communities. Nor is there a tax on what you pay a barber or a beautician, a lawyer, or a doctor. You may be able to buy tickets to a ball game or a rock concert without paying a tax. But if you want to buy the video-

Illinois state income tax A tax paid to the state government that is based on the amount of money an Illinois job holder earns.

Withholding The practice of the government's taking tax money out of each paycheck a wage earner receives. At the end of the year, if the government has taken out too much money, then the wage earner is entitled to a refund. If the government has taken too little, the wage earner must pay the difference between the tax owed and the tax withheld by April 15 — tax day.

W-2 forms Forms that employers send to employees that show how much money they earned in the past year and how much was withheld for state and federal taxes.

Form IL-1040 The form that people who are employed in Illinois use to file their annual tax return. It must be completed and sent to the Illinois Department of Revenue by April 15.

Personal exemption An amount of money a citizen can earn without having to pay income taxes.

Dependent For tax purposes, a dependent is a person who relies on another taxpayer for financial support and/or housing. The state and federal government has rules on who qualifies as a dependent. The rules are based on the dependent person's age, physical abilities, and income. Taxpayers can take deductions for their dependents.

tape of a concert at a music store, expect to pay sales tax.

How about groceries? Surely government would not tax the food on a family's table. Sorry, you are wrong again, although you have hit at one of the touchy points of the state's tax system. Before 1984 the taxes on food and medicine were higher than they are now. But you are still going to pay a one to two percent sales tax on groceries and medicine. But that tax money ends up in the hands of city and county governments — not the state government treasury.

State government taxes other necessities, like electricity, natural gas, and telephone calls. And local governments have the option of imposing their own utility taxes, too.

Income Taxes

If you really want to understand taxes you ought to go into a mall store and apply for a job. Once you are hired, working, and earning money, you really begin to pay taxes. Get a job grilling burgers at the fast food joint in the food court for $6.00 an hour, fifteen hours per week. Imagine that in one year, between January 1 and December 31, you work 50 weeks. You would have $4,500 to spend or save, right?

Wrong. You have to pay income taxes on what you make. Since we're talking about state and local government in this book, we'll concentrate on the **Illinois state income tax**. But you should know that there is a federal income tax on what you earn, too. Fortunately, the Illinois income tax form is simpler to complete than the federal form.

Here's how it works. The state of Illinois, like most states that impose an income tax, is pretty clever. It takes its share of the income tax before you are paid. So from your first $90 paycheck (we'll assume you are paid weekly) it would keep $2.70. This practice is called **withholding**, and under it your employer takes a certain percentage of your salary and ships it off to the Illinois Department of Revenue. This does two things. It saves you from having to make a big tax payment at the end of the year, when you might not have the money. It also ensures that the state gets its money. You can decide which is the more important reason.

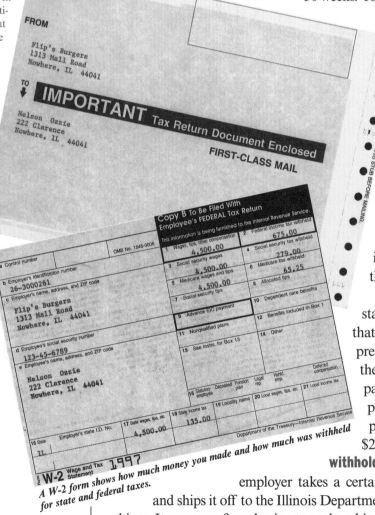

A W-2 form shows how much money you made and how much was withheld for state and federal taxes.

Also withheld from your paycheck are federal income taxes. Your employer sends that money to the U.S. Treasury. And Social Security taxes are also taken out of your pay. That money goes to the U.S. Social Security Administration, which uses the money to make Social Security payments to retired persons. Although today you might prefer to see the cash, the fact that you have made Social Security contributions may someday entitle you to retirement benefits.

Anyway, let's imagine that this goes on all year. Fifty paychecks means fifty $2.70 withholdings that go to the state, or total payments of $135. Sometime the following January your employer will give you a form that shows how much you made, and how much was withheld for state and federal taxes. These **W-2 forms** will have multiple copies, so you can send copies with your federal and state income tax forms.

By April 15, you will be required to file a tax return to the federal and state governments. The return is the means by which you show the government that you have paid (or will pay) your income taxes. As you fill out the tax returns, you will determine how much tax you owe for the year. If the amount of tax you owe is greater than the amount of tax withheld over the course of the year, then you will need to pay more taxes. If, on the other hand, the amount you owe is less than the amount of tax withheld over the year, then you are entitled to receive a tax refund check. The form that you use to report your income taxes to the state government is the **Form IL-1040**.

Illinois lets citizens earn some money before it starts taxing them by giving them a **personal exemption**. For almost 30 years, the amount was $1,000, but beginning in 1998 the governor and state lawmakers increased the amount, in stages, to $2,000.

However, if your parents claim you as a **dependent** on their tax return — and it makes sense for them to do so — you may not be allowed a personal exemption. When your parents claim you as a dependent, you can't claim a personal exemption unless your total income — what you earn plus any interest and dividends — is less than the personal exemption amount.

Except for the question of the personal exemption, the Illinois income tax form is relatively simple. Let's look at a couple examples.

Let's say your total income is $2,200 (that is wages, interest, and the earnings on your college fund) and you get no personal exemption. Multiply your income times 3 percent to determine that you owe $66 in tax. If your employer has withheld $78, you will be due a refund of

Use the Form IL-1040 to file your state income tax return.

$12. Fill out the return, and Illinois will mail you a check for $12.

Alternately, let's say that your total income is $1,100 and that you can claim the personal exemption. When you subtract the exemption from your income, you end up with no income. If your employer has withheld $39, you'll get it all back when you file your state tax return.

Property Taxes: A Local Tax

In 1995 state and local governments in Illinois collected $2,619 in taxes for each person in Illinois. That was $105 higher than the average for the nation. State income taxes in 1995 averaged $450 per person, or about $75 below the U.S. average. But property taxes collected in 1995 averaged $1,003 per person in Illinois, about $229 above the national average. **Property taxes** are based on the value of land and buildings (including homes, factories and stores), and farmland. Property taxes provide much of the money for public schools and for running the governments and providing the services of our cities, villages, counties, townships, and special districts.

Other Ways That State and Local Governments Get Money

Although the government finances its operations primarily through taxes of all sorts, there are other ways that state and local governments can generate the income they need to provide services for the people they serve. One is through grants from the federal government. Another is through money-generating programs like the state lottery. Finally, there are user fees that government entities impose on people who use specific services.

Grants from the Federal Government

Illinois receives funds from the federal government, which provides about one quarter of the money that Illinois state government spends each year. This is not necessarily the blessing that it seems. Most federal money is reimbursement for medical assistance payments made to poor people. If Illinois spends one dollar, it gets 50 cents back from the federal government. The state also gets some federal assistance for roads, job training, and facilities like sewer plants, but all of that spending requires a state spending match.

A Harvard University study showed that Illinois is one of the big losers in terms of federal aid. Because its citizens are relatively wealthy and Illinois houses no major military facilities, Illinoisans contribute $20 billion more in federal taxes than the federal government returns to Illinois in various payments.

The Lottery

One of the best known ways — besides taxes — that the state government has of raising money is through sales of Illinois state lottery tickets. The best proof of the popularity of this state revenue source comes from the long lines of people waiting to buy tickets whenever there is a big jackpot. Each year the lottery earns just over half a billion dollars for Illinois, while returning slightly more than $800 million dollars to winners. Although you hear a lot about the lottery, it is pretty small potatoes when compared to income and sales taxes, which each total about $8.6 billion and $5.8 billion, respectively. Lottery profits account for about three cents of every dollar that the state collects in taxes and fees.

The lottery is supposed to help schools. It does, but not as much as was advertised when the lottery was started back in 1974. Lottery profits all go to elementary and secondary schools, but because of the lottery money, education gets less other state money. It's kind of like trying to fill up a gallon pail with pennies. If you dump in a quart of lottery pennies, then you only need three quarts of other pennies. If you have no lottery pennies you need four quarts of other pennies. Either way, there are only four quarts to the gallon.

Each year the lottery earns just over half a billion dollars for Illinois, while returning slightly more than $800 million dollars to winners.

User Fees

State government also raises money with **user fees**. If you want to camp in a state park, you pay a camping fee. The state uses the money to maintain the park. If you want to go fishing (and you're 16 or over), you buy a fishing license. The state uses the money from fishing licenses to run fish hatcheries to raise fish for you and others to catch. The garbage company pays a fee for each ton of waste dumped in landfills. Those fees are used to pay for recycling programs and to study ways to keep landfills from filling up so fast. And the garbage company, in turn, raises its price so that the person who throws away the garbage ends up paying. If your city has its own garbage trucks, the city will charge a fee or tax to cover the cost.

Note the relationship between the fee and what it is used for. Now you know where the term user fee comes from. The principle is that the person who is using the service should pay the fee. If I hate fish and cannot stand to handle worms, why should I pay taxes to raise fish for you to catch?

Where the Tax Money Goes

There can't be a user fee to cover every service that the government provides. Indeed, some government services benefit everyone. Public schools are an example. Long ago people decided that society benefited from having citizens who could read, write, and do mathematics. In theory, when the state spends money on schools it is investing in its future — the young people who will one day hold jobs and run the government. It would be pretty hard to make children or their parents come up with the $7,170 on average that is spent annually to educate each Illinois elementary and high school student. Citizens of Illinois also want to be safe in their homes, so the state and its cities and counties have police. Imagine how difficult it would be to charge a user fee for calling the police. The same is true of clean air and clean water. Everybody benefits from them, and, through taxes, everybody pays part of the cost.

That is the principle of taxation. Everybody pays a little bit of the cost. The sales tax that you pay when you buy a new CD gets thrown in the hopper with the income taxes your teacher pays and with the profits from this week's Lotto drawing. In the ideal case, no one pays too much and everybody benefits.

About one-fifth of the money that the state spends comes from the sales tax, one quarter comes from the state income tax, and another one quarter comes from the federal government. The rest comes from an assortment of other taxes on things including gasoline, cigarettes, liquor, telephone calls, and horse racing bets.

How Your Tax Dollars Are Spent

Taxes get spent for a variety of things. In 1999, for example, about 26 cents of each dollar of state taxes was spent on education — for elementary and high schools, public universities and college financial aid. About 13 cents of each dollar was spent on transportation, primarily roads and bridges but also airports, bus systems, and trains. About 16 cents of each dollar was spent on various welfare programs, and 18 cents of each dollar was spent for health and human services. Smaller amounts were spent on environmental protection, state police, and prison systems.

Too Much Taxes?

In the real world, most people think they pay too many taxes. The late Maurice Scott, who served as president of the Taxpayers' Federation of Illinois, used to open talks by saying he had found the ideal tax. A tax on hair oil (an old-fashioned kind of styling gel). Mr. Scott nearly always got a laugh from the crowd when he said this because he was bald.

Because taxes are unpopular, politicians are wary about raising taxes. They always have been. In fact, you might be surprised to know that while the federal government started taxing income in 1913, the state of Illinois didn't charge an income tax until 1969. That year, newly elected Governor Richard B. Ogilvie championed — and pushed through the General Assembly — the first income tax in Illinois. It was a tough action for the governor to take. Ogilvie's reward? Three years later he was defeated when he ran for reelection, and his income tax program was a major campaign issue. Even today, if you listen carefully to pre-election political ads on the radio and TV, you'll notice that one candidate, sometimes both, will be trying to convince voters that his or her opponent is (or will be) guilty of raising taxes.

Elected officials often end up being torn between those who want more government services and those who want lower taxes. State legislators are elected to do things, and they like to bring projects home to their districts. Those projects include new roads and bridges, a new runway at the local airport, state money for a program to fight teen pregnancy, and new storm

---

How a Tax Dollar Got Spent in 1999

13¢ for transportation

16¢ for welfare programs

18¢ for health and human services

26¢ for schools

27¢ for all other services

A Bullfighting Arena in Peoria

The legislators who govern Illinois are faced with a constant dilemma. They would like to provide people with newer and better services, but those newer and better services will often raise taxes. That dilemma produces another characteristic of state tax increases. To justify a tax increase, legislators usually have to use the new money to pay for a little something for everybody.

Where in the Peoria skyline would you put a domed bullfighting ring?

Say, for example, that the city of Peoria decided to become the bullfighting capital of North America. Say also that the city's economic planners have made a convincing case that they could attract millions of tourists to Peoria if they had year-round bullfighting in a covered bullfighting arena. The tourists would occupy hotel rooms, eat in local restaurants, buy gasoline, and shop in the stores. All this activity would provide jobs for Peorians and new tax revenue for local and state governments.

The problem is that Peoria would need a covered bullfighting ring, a $200 million expense for which the city doesn't have the money. So, it is proposed that the state pay half the cost and raise that money through an 11 cent per-pack increase in the cigarette tax. To provide the money for the Peoria bullfighting ring, state legislators must pass a law to raise the cigarette tax.

For the three legislators from Peoria — one state senator and two state representatives — that would be a pretty easy vote. Those three legislators could tell their constituents that they have to pay higher cigarette taxes to build this new facility. It is much more difficult for the other 58 state senators and 116 state representatives. The higher cigarette taxes may anger voters in Chicago, Alton, and Urbana, who believe they are paying higher taxes for Peoria's ben-efit. If they get mad enough, they may vote against their state legislators in the next election.

So, it is unlikely that legislators will raise the state cigarette tax to build something just for Peoria. Far more likely is the prospect that they would raise the cigarette tax five cents or ten cents and fund a series of projects across the state so Chicago might get a new hockey arena, Alton a dog racing track, and Effingham a new stock car race track at the same time Peoria gets its bullfighting arena.

When it comes time to raise taxes, both how the money is spent and who pays the new tax are important. In 1997, the General Assembly was looking for ways to increase school funding. There are schools in every legislative district, so there was no big issue there. But, there was much consternation over whom to tax. Several commissions had recommended raising the individual income tax, but lawmakers balked at that. Instead, they approved a package that increased taxes on cigarettes, phone calls, and riverboat casinos.

In 1999, newly elected Governor George Ryan propsed Illinois First, a $12 billion program to build roads, repair schools, and modernize transit systems. Lawmakers passed higher liquor taxes and increased license plate fees to fund the program, after the governor convinced them that benefits would flow to their home districts. ∎

SUM IT UP

So, if you're alive and in Illinois, it's a pretty safe bet that you cannot escape taxes. In this state (as in most others) you'll run into:

- Gas taxes (as well as taxes on other items)
- Sales taxes
- Income taxes
- Property taxes.

For state and local governments, taxes are a source of income. Along with taxes, state and local governments can receive income through:

- Grants from the federal government
- The lottery
- User fees.

Why do state and local governments need money from the people? Because it is up to them to provide the services people want: schools, roads, parks, clean air, police and fire protection, and the other services we've come to expect from the government.

This need to gather and spend money often puts elected officials (as well as every thinking citizen) in a bind. For every new or improved service that people can get from the government, there is a cost that is usually paid through increased taxes or user fees. Through our legislators we are constantly having to find the right balance between the benefits of government services and the costs we pay to enjoy them. ■

To find out more...
start with the *Governing Illinois* web site at **www.uis.edu/govern**

sewers for an area that is being flooded. Citizens want these services, but, at the same time, the same citizens as voters often object to new taxes.

Too Few Services?

Although no one likes to pay more taxes, plenty of people want new or expanded services from government. Visit the state Capitol in May if you want to see who. Almost daily there are rallies by groups who want the state to start new programs or spend more money on what it already does. A group of homeless people may be camped on the lawn to illustrate the need for more money for housing. College students may be arguing for more state tax money for universities so that they do not have to pay higher tuition. Hospital workers may be demanding higher state payments for treating Illinoisans on welfare. The people who want more services from state government often argue that state taxes in Illinois are low. They are right.

The people who do not depend on state services often argue that in Illinois taxes are high. They are right, too. In Illinois the state taxes, particularly state income taxes, are low. But taxes by local governments are high. This situation exists, in part, because state government does not pay its constitutionally mandated share of public education costs, forcing school districts and their property taxpayers to make up the difference. However, the low state taxes and high local taxes balance off, leaving Illinois' tax burden around the average for the United States.

Although tax increase votes are difficult ones for legislators, rest assured that from time to time taxes will be raised or new taxes imposed. Some, like the tax on a new Porsche, are very conspicuous. Others, like the gasoline tax, are inconspicuous. But nobody can escape them, not even a teenager hanging around the mall on a Saturday in early spring. ■

Chapter 9

Springfield teen, Jennifer Esslinger, campaign volunteer, goes door to door soliciting support for city council candidate Dawn DeFraties.

Getting Involved: Your Influence on Governing Illinois

by Laura Ryan and Ed Wojcicki

A woman running for alderman, going door to door on her first try for the city council, made a routine knock on the door one wintry day in Springfield. She politely explained why she wanted the posi-

Citizen A person who, by birth or choice, is a legal member of a nation. A citizen owes allegiance to the government of that nation, is entitled to certain rights and privileges, and must meet certain obligations.

tion, handed out a flier, and left, heading toward the neighbor's house.

Realizing how cold it was, the woman inside the house told her grade-school age daughter, "Let me pour her a cup of coffee, and you go and give it to her. It's not easy to be campaigning on such a cold day."

The girl ran outside and found the candidate two doors up the street. The candidate was surprised to be met by such hospitality, and she gratefully accepted the coffee. It was the girl's first exposure to a candidate on the campaign trail. It left a lasting impression on both the girl and the candidate, who not only won that aldermanic seat, but a few years later also ran successfully for a seat in the Illinois House of Representatives. The family and that state rep remain in contact with each other and occasionally recall in conversations how a cup of coffee started a good relationship between a few citizens and a public official.

And, as for the girl, when she got into high school, she jumped at a chance to run for the student council, and later she went on to become student body president in her senior year.

Government does provide valuable services, such as snow removal during winter storms. But you should think of yourself as much more than a consumer of government services. As a citizen, you have many responsibilities.

So What? Does it Matter?

Some important questions haven't yet been asked in this book. They are these: So what? Why do you need to know all this information about state and local government? Does it matter? And, what can you do about it, anyway?

The answer is simple: Plenty.

There is plenty you can do, should do, and must do, because our system of representative democracy is based on the premise that we can govern ourselves and that, in fact, we want to govern ourselves. That means you cannot leave it up to everybody else to make all the decisions and do all the governing.

Unfortunately, confidence in government officials at the turn of this century is not high. Many citizens believe they can no longer make a difference. They think they cannot affect what public officials do or how they might vote on important issues. Stories about scandals in government and the vast amounts of money contributed to candidates by interest groups, unions, and corporations feed citizens' perception that our government is less and less a government "of the people." Indeed, Mike Lawrence, who was Governor Jim Edgar's press secretary, has said that, from his perspective, the special interest groups are deeply engaged in the process of decision-making, but not enough ordinary people are engaged.

You can change that. You have the power and many opportunities to make a difference.

While many citizens use the services that government provides, polls indicate that Americans of all ages are becoming more cynical about their government. Many have forgotten it is their government. They perceive "the government" as some unknown people "out there" who are out of touch with them and maybe out of touch with reality. The number of Americans who vote regularly is on the decline, and typically fewer than half of the people between the ages of 18 and 24 vote regularly. Once again, you can change that. You can make a difference in an important way once you turn 18, just by registering to vote and showing up at your polling place on election day.

The Responsibilities of Citizenship

Many citizens perceive governments as institutions whose primary responsibilities are to provide them with services, such as building and repairing roads, collecting the garbage once a week, and making sure the sewer system does not back up during a rainstorm. Too many citizens judge their government by the quality of services they provide. To a certain extent, there is nothing wrong with this, because a government does provide valuable services, as do private businesses such as auto repair shops, video rental stores, and fitness centers.

But as a citizen, you should perceive yourself as much more than a consumer of government services. As a **citizen** in a society that has a represen-

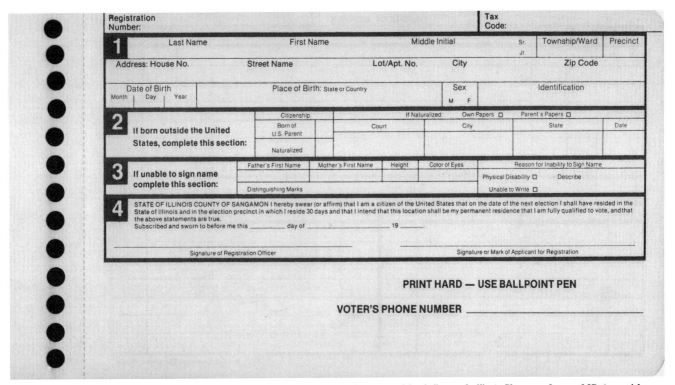

Registering to vote is simple. Find an official registrar. (There's always one at the nearest driver's license facility). Show two forms of ID (one with your picture). Fill out this short form. And boom! You're a registered voter.

tative form of government, you have many responsibilities as well as many rights.

Register to Vote. Then Vote!

It is very easy to register to vote. All you need are two forms of identification — one with your picture on it. For many people this will be a driver's license. The other form of identification might be a school ID card or a recent piece of mail with your name and address on it to prove where you live.

There are many places where you can register to vote. You can go to any state driver's license facility and register there. Or you can call the elections office at the county clerk's office in the courthouse of the county where you live. In many places, people know who the **precinct committeeman or committeewoman** is in their neighborhood, and most committeemen or committeewomen are happy to drop by your house with a voter registration form. Some high schools make it very easy by having official registrars on the staff who can help students register to vote at their high school when they turn 18. And some public libraries have registrars as well. Registering to vote is a must for anyone over 18 who wants to be a good citizen.

Voting is a constitutional right. Early in American history only White men over the age of 21 could vote. Then it took two constitutional amendments – one in 1870 and the other in 1920 – to give Black people and women, respectively, the right to vote. Then, when Americans 18 and older were in the military and fighting in Vietnam, the thinking finally prevailed that if young people were old enough to die for their country, they surely were old enough to vote. So in 1971, the Twenty-Sixth Amendment to the U.S. Constitution gave 18-year-olds the right to vote.

On voting day you will sign in at the polling place in your precinct. An election judge will check to see that your registration is in order, and then you will be given a ballot to take into the booth with you.

You should cherish and value this right, and consider it a responsibility.

You might even consider, as a class project, organizing a voter registration drive at your school or in your neighborhood. And be on the lookout for other groups that are sponsoring voter registration drives. In the fall of 1998, for example, the Pilsen East Planning Association hosted a voter registration drive for neighborhood residents. More than 75 people stopped by and more than 50 registered, giving more voting power to their community.

But you can't stop at registration. You then have to vote. Vote in all the elections. Presidential elections usually get the highest turnout of voters in the United States, but it is important to vote in your local elections, too, because your local governments can affect issues you know about: bicycle trails, curbside recycling, traffic lights and other local road projects, even laws limiting the use of your skateboard.

Other Options for Citizen Involvement

Voting is just one of your responsibilities as a citizen. Probably not enough attention is given today to what it means to be a citizen. The U.S. is often identified as having an individualized society. That means many Americans pay close attention to what is important to them personally, what is of benefit to them, and what will help them get more of what they want. It is good for people to seek personal fulfillment, but, as a citizen in a democracy, you also should have concerns about what is best for your community. In fact, being a citizen assumes that you will

be active in your community in some way. "Ask not what your country can do for you," President John F. Kennedy said in his famous inaugural address. "Ask what you can do for your country."

At the beginning of this chapter we said that there are many opportunities for you to become actively involved in governmental activities at the local, state, or federal levels. Let's take a look at some now. Some that we will discuss are educational projects, aimed at getting you and your family better informed. Others enable you to have a direct influence on laws that might be passed or on the outcome of elections.

Lawmakers do respond to citizens — even young ones. Here, state Senator Barack Obama of Chicago takes time to visit an elementary school class.

Find Out Who Represents You and Make Contact

Find out what precinct, ward, legislative, and congressional districts you live in. Find out who represents you in local, state, and national governments. Perhaps a parent, neighbor, or teacher can help you. Much of this information is now available on the Internet. Then make a list. Write down their names, addresses, phone numbers, and e-mail addresses. You also should know the names of your two United States senators and your representative in the U.S. Congress. At the local level, the titles of your officials will vary depending on where you live. But find out the name of your mayor, village president, or city manager, and find out the name of your alderman, village board member, or city council member. These people represent you, and if you know the names of all of these people, you will have a lot more information than many of your fellow citizens.

Then, don't be shy about writing or calling these people. If you want information about an issue, just ask for it. If you already have an opinion, express it clearly and be sure to support your position with facts. Specifically ask your elected officials whether they agree or disagree with you, and why. Never be satisfied with a polite letter that thanks you for expressing your opinion and promises to take your views into consideration. Write again, and ask again what the official thinks about an issue and how he or she intends to vote. Include a return address so your lawmaker can respond to your letter.

You may think that your voice won't be heard, but, when enough citizens express their views, legislators do pay attention. Many elected officials tally how many letters and phone calls they receive on various issues, and what their **constituents** think about each issue. Many lawmakers say that they receive very few letters or phone calls about many issues. So your letter or phone call can make a huge difference, and if you can get your friends to write to the same officials about the same topic, your influence can be even greater. Your opinion might be in the minority, but don't let that stop you from expressing it. Citizen pressure does help legislators make decisions on how to vote on issues, and, sometimes, what officials perceive today as a bad idea eventually becomes tomorrow's great idea as more information becomes known, or public opinion changes.

Get involved in your own student government at school. This subcommittee of the student council at Pekin Community High School is making plans to host the Senior Citizens' Prom, an annual event that brings students and seniors together for a night out.

Stay Informed

Stay informed by reading newspapers and magazines, paying attention to news on radio and television, and watching programs on C-SPAN or MSNBC and similar channels. You might find some of this boring. But remember that, as a citizen, you should spend some time keeping up with what your government officials are doing.

Get Involved in Student Government

Get involved in your own student government at school. While this is not officially part of our representative form of government called for by the U.S. and Illinois constitutions, student government is important too. Pay attention to what your student council does, and make suggestions to your class representatives. If all the students believe something at your school can be changed, going through the student government is one way to seek that change. Of course, you can become even more active and run for one of the offices.

Attend a Local Meeting

Attend a city council, village board, or school board meeting in your own community. In Chicago, you should consider attending a local school council meeting. You will probably see and hear some things that surprise you, such as the formal processes that these groups use to make their decisions. You might also be surprised, though, to hear them talking about issues or a part of your community that you already know something about. Maybe they will discuss putting up a stoplight at a busy intersection, or making some improvements to a park near your house. This is local government, and it affects you. Many communities now broadcast their village board or city council meetings on cable television. If your class ever attends a meeting as a class project, you'll probably be surprised by the recognition you receive from the mayor or board members.

Join a Political Party

At some point you might decide that one political party best represents your own views and interests. Political parties make nominations for president, members of Congress, governor, legislators, statewide elected officials, and sometimes local officials. In Illinois, you have to declare your party in the primary elections, but not the general elections. You may find that neither the Republicans nor the Democrats represent all of your personal views exactly. So you might consider choosing the one closest to your views. Some counties have separate organizations of Young Democrats and Young Republicans.

Or, you may find yourself more comfortable being officially independent, or getting involved in other political parties, such as the Libertarians, the United Party, or (in Chicago) the Harold Washington Party. "Third parties" — parties other than the Democrats or Republicans — generally have not been effective in getting people elected to office, but they do play a role in the public discussion of issues and therefore have a legitimate place in our governmental processes.

If you volunteer to work on a political campaign, you will initially have to pay your dues by running errands, making routine telephone calls, or preparing envelopes.

Work in Political Campaigns

If you decide to join a political party, you should seek your Republican or Democrat precinct committeeman or committeewoman and offer your services to help in election campaigns. Or, contact the staff of a candidate you like. All campaign staffs from the presidential level down to the local elections need volunteer helpers. Don't expect to be put in a position of great responsibility and influence right away. Realize that you will have to "pay your dues" by doing simple tasks. You may get started by running errands, preparing envelopes, or making routine telephone calls. Or, you might be asked to help put up yard signs, hand out fliers by going door to door, helping at fundraisers and receptions, or organizing mailings.

How Students Can Get Involved – Right Now!

Because many officials and groups are concerned about getting young people interested in government, it is not surprising that a number of programs have emerged that involve high school and college students. Just a sampling of them are mentioned here.

- **Kids Voting USA.** One highlight of this program is that young people go to real polling places with their parents on election day and cast ballots in the Kids Voting booths. Different organizations sponsor the program in local communities, and the results of the kids' votes usually get some publicity. Kids Voting USA provides a curriculum for grades K-12. For high school students, the curriculum includes a scavenger hunt for items such as yard signs, political brochures, stickers, pins, and other items. It also asks students to identify the top ten campaign issues, each candidate's position on the issues, and the top ten political action committees that support the candidates.

- **The Mikva Challenge Grant Program.** This is named after Abner and Zoe Mikva. Abner Mikva was a state representative, congressman, judge and White House counsel. This program, administered by the League of Women Voters of Illinois, provides grants to Chicago area high schools to teach students about the electoral process. Teachers assist interns who choose to volunteer in a real campaign and become totally engaged in the process. Enriching the experience are three program meetings featuring high-profile public officials or former public officials, who encourage the students to participate in the electoral process. Students participate a minimum of 20 hours in the program.

- **The Dirksen Congressional Center.** While this is not a specific program, the Pekin-based center is named after one of Illinois' most revered public officials, the late Senator Everett Dirksen. The center's web site – **www.congresslink.org** – is one of the most thorough, easy-to-navigate online resources to help students and teachers understand Congress and the U.S. government in great detail. You can type your Zip Code into a search engine and come up with pictures and information about your U.S. senators and your representative.

- **Official State of Illinois Web Site.** We cannot resist listing this web site here, because **www.state.il.us** is a wonderful place to begin learning about state government. It lists information about state officials, tourism, state parks, and much more. There is even a section "For Kids," which is a bit childish for high school students but nonetheless a fun site for anyone who wants to get a better idea of how government is using technology to interact with citizens of all ages. A state law requires the Illinois State Library to provide an official web site with a lot of information about state government, and this web site was in the development stages as this book went to the printer. Go to this textbook's site, **www.uis.edu/govern**, for the latest information. ∎

Whatever job you do, you are learning more about the system, and, at the same time, getting to know politicians and party leaders. They are getting to know you, too, so, if you ever have an interest in running for office as a representative of your party, it will be helpful that party leaders already know you.

Do Community Service

More and more high schools are requiring some community service as a requirement for graduation. Doing volunteer service for some organizations is not governmental service, but it is service that makes a good contribution to the community and helps you understand your community's needs more fully. Somebody once said that service is the rent we pay for our room on this earth. Examples of places you might volunteer are at nursing homes, crisis nurseries, women's shelters, local breadlines or food pantries, hospitals, after-school programs that need tutors or baby-sitters, Habitat for Humanity, the Boy Scouts and Girl Scouts, the YMCA/YWCA, or places

Many interest groups hold rallies in Springfield to make legislators aware of their concerns. Not all are as flamboyant as this volunteer from People for the Ethical Treatment of Animals (PETA), who drew some stares from passersby during the spring of 1999.

that serve your neighborhood in specialized ways. Studies indicate that when more people participate in any form of community activity or group — in other words, the more "civically engaged" a community is — the stronger the democracy is. Therefore, your community involvement strengthens our democracy.

Volunteer for an Interest Group

Besides volunteering for a political party, you can also get involved with an interest group that is trying to affect government policy. Some schools have Students Against Driving Drunk chapters, for example. And if you ask around, read the newspaper, or check out the Internet, you will discover that many groups hold occasional rallies you might want to attend. On sensitive issues where Americans are deeply divided, groups on both sides of the issue are usually organized, need volunteers, and hold occasional rallies. Such issues include gun rights, abortion, the death penalty, gay rights, environmental policy, and many more. It is usually easy to find information about such groups, and many of them actively seek "members" to do volunteer work, write elected officials, and contribute money.

Sign Up for the Selective Service System

The U.S. military stopped drafting Americans into military service in 1973. But, federal law requires virtually all males to sign up for the Selective Service System within 30 days after they become 18 years old, just in case circumstances change and the draft would be reinstituted. Male citizens and male aliens from 18 to 25 years old living in the U.S. must register. There are few exceptions.

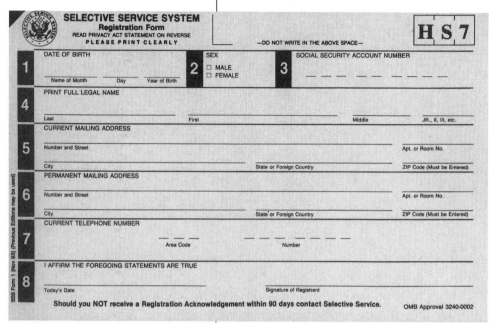

Virtually all males must sign up for the Selective Service System within 30 days after they turn 18.

Most people receive a card in the mail to alert them that registering is necessary. You may complete the requirement for registering by returning that card. Or you can register at any post office, over the Internet, or at your high school if it has a teacher certified as a Selective Service Registrar. Failure to register is a felony, and may disqualify you from receiving financial aid for college or holding a government job.

Do Some Bill Tracking

You can see how bills in the Illinois General Assembly are making their way through the legislative process that we talked about in chapter 4. You can get started by reading the newspaper and selecting a topic of interest that has been introduced in legislation. Or visit the General Assembly's web site (www.legis.state.il.us) and search for a bill with a topic of interest to you. You can call your legislator's office and ask the legislator to send an official copy of the bill to you. Then, make periodic calls to find out to which committee the bill has been assigned, when (and if) the committee will conduct a hearing on the bill, whether (or when) the committee will vote on the bill, and so on. This can get complicated because some bills get amended many times, or they may be replaced in favor of a similar bill either from the House or Senate. Follow the bill either until it reaches the governor's desk, or — as happens with many bills — until a committee votes it down or lets it die by not considering it.

Tour Government Buildings

Take a walking tour of government buildings, such as county courthouses, village halls and city halls, your county jail, or state government buildings, whether in your home county, Springfield, Chicago, or other cities. Some classes or schools routinely take groups of students to Springfield or Washington, D.C., to get a firsthand look at their government. You can make arrangements in advance to meet with your own elected representatives when you are in those cities.

Hold Mock Elections and Class Debates

You or your classmates can play the roles of candidates. Announce the results of student elections to the entire school.

Write Letters to the Editor

Your local newspapers appreciate thoughtful letters about public policy issues. Being involved means expressing your opinion. What do you think about the state's zero-tolerance law that affects teens' right to drive, or attempts to censor Internet access or communication? Do you agree with the U.S. Supreme Court's decision that flag-burning is a legitimate form of protest? Do you feel offended by it, or do you agree that the ruling protects your rights under the First Amendment? You may have strong feelings on the issues of abortion and gun control, too. What do you think of the ideas of withholding a student's driver's license if he or she drops out of school? All of these topics are controversial, and arguments will be heard and decisions will be made by the people who represent you in the state and federal legislatures.

Most newspapers publish letters from readers about these and other topics when they are in the news. But don't just write. Read the letters written by other people in your community. That is one way to find out what they are thinking.

Some classes or schools routinely take groups of students to Springfield to get a firsthand look at their government.

Surf the Internet and Find Political Chat Rooms

Create and participate in electronic chat rooms on specific political topics via the Internet with students at other schools either in your own community or elsewhere in the state or nation. The web site created for this book – www.uis.edu/govern – can become your starting point because it provides many links to information about your government and how you can be a more active citizen.

Students in Government: Interns and Pages

College students — and to a lesser degree, high school students — have opportunities for internships in state government, either through their university or college or through one of several government agencies. You can contact state agencies such as the Illinois Environmental Protection Agency, the Illinois Department of Transportation, or Central Management Services to find out what kinds of internships they offer either during the

Craig Smith, an intern with the Illinois Governmental Internship Program, works closely with his boss, Springfield state Senator Larry Bomke.

school year or in the summer. College graduates can apply for one of several internship programs that are part of a graduate program, such as the Legislative Staff Internship Program, in which the student works for the staff of one of the legislative leaders, or the Graduate Public Service Internship Program at the University of Illinois at Springfield.

For high school students, the Illinois Governmental Internship Program provides an opportunity for about 20 high school seniors a year to take a semester's sabbatical from all their regular studies and serve as special assistants to senior officials in state government in Springfield. The students live with a Springfield family during this time, and the program's success is based on a close one-on-one relationship with a high-ranking official.

Also, both the U.S. Congress and the Illinois General Assembly employ a small number of teenagers as pages. Pages are messengers for the legislators when they are in session. You can contact your U.S. congressman or congresswoman or state representative or senator about this opportunity.

Check the *Governing Illinois* web site for up-to-date contact information if you are interested in these internship possibilities.

For Jim Edgar an Internship Was the Start of Something Big

Jim Edgar had an early interest in politics and government, and his career provides a great example of how taking advantage of early opportunities can lead to even bigger opportunities.

As early as grade school Edgar had an interest in politics, and he got involved in a mock election in which he helped Dwight Eisenhower receive the most presidential votes.

Later in life, Edgar became student body president at Eastern Illinois University. Then, after graduating, he was accepted into the Legislative Staff Internship program in Springfield in 1968. He still lists this internship experience among the most significant events of his life, because it directed him to a career in state government. The young Edgar worked on the staff of the Senate Republicans during his internship and later said it gave him an inside look at how government works. That internship also led to jobs on Senate and House legislative staffs in Springfield. The first time Edgar ran for the Illinois House, he lost. But he later won two terms in the Illinois House, worked on Governor James Thompson's staff, served as secretary of state for 10 years, and then became Illinois' 38th governor in 1991.

So internships and other opportunities for students can be wonderful ways for students to get some practical experience and make valuable contacts that lead to bigger and better things. ∎

Careers in Public Service

Millions of jobs in the United States are with the national, state, or local government. This may surprise you until you consider that many teaching and law enforcement jobs, and many nursing, legal, and scientific jobs as well as secretarial positions involve work in some unit of government. So do jobs involving kitchen help and maintenance work. So, whether you are interested in medicine, teaching, journalism, biology, the environment, social work, counseling, cooking, or many other fields, keep in mind that going to work for a governmental agency could become one of your options. Also, construction jobs often depend on government contracts for buildings and highway projects, and, thus, these workers are indirectly compensated by government. The benefits and pension programs of many public-sector jobs are attractive to many people, which is another reason they choose a career in public service.

According to information published in 1998 by the Illinois Department of Commerce and Community Affairs, the largest employer in the state of Illinois is the State of Illinois. Many of these jobs are in the civil service system, for which a person must take a test to qualify for the many levels of positions. Those with the required qualifications who score highly on the examinations have their name placed on a list of people eligible for interviews. Some professional positions are outside of the civil service system, and no qualifying exam is required. However, applicants must meet the professional qualifications to be considered. For some positions in state government, it is helpful to have a political sponsor, such as a member of the General Assembly or a local political leader, to speak on one's behalf.

You don't have to be a politician to have a career in government. Here, an engineer hired by the Illinois Department of Central Management Services ensures that construction plans are up to code so that this new building will be structurally sound.

Even if you are not a government employee, another argument for understanding government has to do with employment. Nearly all businesses are affected by local, state, or federal regulations in some way. Where you want to locate your business, for example, will be affected by local zoning regulations. Many business people argue that government should have fewer laws because the costs associated with complying with tax regulations, health and safety statutes, and building codes — to name a few examples — can eat into a business's profits. On the other hand, others argue for additional laws and regulations to protect workers. The government also will issue certificates allowing only qualified people to pursue selected careers. Teachers, doctors, tavern owners, hairdressers, tattoo artists, truck drivers, and operators of bingo games are just a few examples of occupations licensed by the state of Illinois.

Many jobs are created when laws are passed. For example, thousands

SUM IT UP

The point of this chapter isn't to prepare you to take tests and pass a social studies course. The purpose is to prepare you to take on the responsibility of citizenship. Remember that:

1. You are a citizen, not merely a consumer of government services. This means, for starters, that you should register to vote when you turn 18. And then exercise that right to vote.

2. Your elected officials are available to talk to you. You can call them, write them, or visit them to let them know what you think about public policy issues. You might be surprised at how accessible your elected officials are.

3. There are many ways that you can be engaged in the government and in the community. You don't have to do them all, but you should do something.

4. You can consider working for the government as a career. Many people do, because the government needs workers and professional staff with many kinds of expertise.

5. You are a citizen for life; therefore, your commitment to learning about government should never waver. Issues will change and new ones will emerge as the years go on, but the process never stops. Be a participant, not an observer.

6. You can stay current on many of the ideas and programs mentioned in this chapter by accessing the *Governing Illinois* web site: www.uis.edu/govern. ■

To find out more...
start with the *Governing Illinois* web site at **www.uis.edu/govern**

of employment opportunities exist because of the laws protecting the environment. In addition to government jobs in agencies such as the Environmental Protection Agency, new companies have started up, creating more jobs, to handle such things as recycling products and removing asbestos from old buildings.

Becoming a Lifelong Participant and Student-Citizen of Government

Once you have gone to work, you may have the opportunity to get involved in the political activity of your union, professional, or business organization. You may not want to work in politics as a profession, but you should always stay involved. Be ready to participate in rallies or demonstrations, write letters, make phone calls, sign petitions, and donate a little money to support causes in which you believe.

Your involvement in government should never stop. You will learn about government as a student and participate in some ways, but you will have lifelong opportunities to communicate with government officials, become one yourself, and stay abreast of what is happening at the local, state, national, and international levels. So you'll never stop learning, and you'll always be a citizen with that precious right to vote.

The issues may change. When the 20th century began, some of the biggest issues centered on getting healthier environments for workers in dirty factories. In the 1930s the Great Depression dominated the political scene, and in the 1940s the focus was on World War II. The civil rights movement caught fire in the 1950s and reached new highs in the 1960s and 1970s, when the Vietnam War and the Watergate scandal changed the nature of American politics forever. At the turn of the 21st century, some of the biggest issues are what to do with an aging baby boomer generation, the soaring costs of health care and welfare, and lingering inequities in the workplace for women and minorities. Some of the specific issues that are likely to be topics of debate are affirmative action, Social Security, and assisted suicide.

You are a citizen; therefore, you should be involved in issues of interest to you. But remember, you have a lot of competition and not everyone will agree with your positions, even when you are absolutely certain you are right. Sometimes you will want to stick to your opinion as a matter of principle. Other times it is wise to be prepared to compromise and adjust your objectives to ones that are important and achievable, with give-and-take on your part and on the part of those who disagree with you at first. So don't expect to get everything you want from the government in the legislative and electoral processes. Remember that politics is the art of compromise, and, as an active citizen, you serve your community by having an impact on decisions elected officials make. ■

Index

About the
Institute for Public Affairs

Because of its location in the state capital, the University of Illinois at Springfield has a special mission in public affairs. To fulfill its mission, the campus directs educational, research, and service efforts to help solve problems facing the state and nearby local communities. The Institute for Public Affairs is a primary vehicle through which the campus carries out these public affairs activities.

The Institute for Public Affairs houses the Springfield campus's major public affairs units: the Center for Legal Studies, the Graduate Public Service Internship Program, *Illinois Issues*, the Illinois Legislative Studies Center, the Office of Policy and Administrative Studies, the Survey Research Office, the Television Office, and radio stations WUIS/WIPA. These units are coordinated by the Institute's Central Office.

In cooperation with Institute for Public Affairs' Editorial Board, the Institute also oversees the publication and dissemination of works designed to enhance citizen awareness of issues, policy, and the history of Illinois government. Members of the editorial board are:

Glen Hahn Cope
School of Public Affairs and Administration, University of Illinois at Springfield

Peggy Boyer Long
Illinois Issues *magazine, University of Illinois at Springfield*

Richard J. Martin
University of Illinois Press, University of Illinois at Urbana-Champaign

Therese McGuire
Institute of Government and Public Affairs, University of Illinois at Urbana-Champaign

Patrick O'Grady
Legislative Research Unit

Jack Van Der Slik
Director and professor emeritus, Illinois Legislative Studies Center, University of Illinois at Springfield

Peter Wenz
Philosophy and Legal Studies Departments, University of Illinois at Springfield

Edward R. Wojcicki
Institute Publications, University of Illinois at Springfield
(ex-officio member and chair)

About the Authors

James M. Banovetz is professor emeritus of political science at Northern Illinois University in DeKalb. He is a member and former chair of the *Illinois Issues* magazine board. He has lectured on state and local government throughout the United States and in Europe, Africa, and Asia. During his professorial career, he served as faculty advisor/director to a large percentage of Illinois' city managers while they were pursuing their professional education.

Patrick J. Burns is a retired counselor and humanities instructor. He taught at Shelbyville High School for 34 years. He still teaches social studies part-time for Lake Land Community College in Mattoon. A graduate of Southern Illinois University at Carbondale, he received his B.S. in 1957 and his M.S. in 1959. He has done other graduate work at the University of Missouri, Eastern Illinois University, Illinois State University, and the University of Illinois. He credits much of his understanding of Illinois state government to his family's discussions when he was growing up in the coal mining area of Williamson County, particularly from his aunt, Agnes Burns Wieck, and her husband, Edward Wieck.

The late **Darlene Emmert Fisher** was a social studies teacher at New Trier Township High School in Winnetka (1963-69, 1979-90). She also taught eighth grade social studies at St. Francis Xavier School in Wilmette (1975-76). She received her A.B. in 1962 from Albion College and her M.A. in 1963 from the University of Pennsylvania. She was a member of the board of the League of Women Voters of Evanston. She published several articles in various periodicals, including a biweekly column for the *Evanston Review* (1979-82). Her contributions to the first edition of *Governing Illinois* remain as the foundation for chapter 7 and the case study at the end of chapter 2.

Michael D. Klemens is the manager of policy and communications for the Illinois Department of Revenue. Before that, he served as Statehouse bureau chief for *Illinois Issues* magazine from 1986 to 1992. He taught eighth grade English and social studies in New York at Ogdensburg Free Academy (1972-73). He received his A.B. from Dartmouth College in 1971 and his M.A. from Sangamon State University in 1986. He lives in Springfield.

Eleanor Meyer retired from Beardstown Junior High School after 30 years of teaching geography and U.S. history. She received her B.A. from George Washington University in 1956 and her M.A. from Western Illinois University in 1982. She lives in Beardstown and currently teaches a GED class for Lincoln Land Community College.

Laura Ryan teaches at Springfield High School. She has taught twelfth grade American government for six years. She received her B.A. in social science education from Eastern Illinois University in 1993 and her M.A. in child family and community services from the University of Illinois at Springfield in 1997.

Denny L. Schillings has been a social studies teacher at Homewood-Flossmoor High School since 1973. Before that, he taught at Sheldon High School and Edwards County High School in Albion. He received his A.A. from Wabash Valley College in Mount Carmel in 1967, his B.S. in education from Eastern Illinois University in 1969, his M.A. in history from Eastern Illinois University in 1972, and an M.A. in administration from Governors State University in 1995. He has also done post-graduate work at Chicago State University, Illinois State University, and Northern Illinois University. He is the author of *The Living Constitution*, published by Glencoe/McGraw-Hill Publishing Co. (1997) and has been contributor, consultant, or editor for other publications on history, social studies, and economics. He is affiliated with several professional associations, and, in 1993-94, he served as the president of the National Council for the Social Studies.

Judy Lee (Lewis) Uphoff is the principal of Lovington High School, after having taught social studies for twenty years. She received her B.S. in education in 1969 and her M.S. in education in 1972, both from Eastern Illinois University. She is a contributing author to *Understanding the Illinois Constitution*, published by the Illinois Bar Foundation in 1986, and she was a government intern for Illinois state Rep. Mike Tate.

Ed Wojcicki is publisher of *Illinois Issues* magazine and director of Institute Publications in the Institute for Public Affairs at the University of Illinois at Springfield. As a former reporter and editor, he covered government at all levels, and he spent one summer during college as a congressional intern in Washington, D.C. He has a journalism degree from the University of Missouri and has done graduate studies in political science at the University of Illinois at Springfield.